Dare to
EVOLVE

Sustainable Solutions to Reframe Our Mindset from Striving to Thriving

Don McClure

Dare to Evolve
Sustainable Solutions to Reframe Our Mindset
from Striving to Thriving

by Don McClure
Copyright © 2025 Don McClure
Publisher: JenRich Press
Website: www.daretoevolve.us
Contact through the website for permission requests, speaking arrangements, and wholesale inquiries.

Disclaimer
The author is not an expert in any of the topics covered herein and as such the information in this book is meant to educate and further discussions that will enable sustainable solutions. There is no claim that the information in this book will enable any purpose, only that we as a species need to seek better solutions for potentially better outcomes than we are currently experiencing. These examples of solutions that seem to be working for a number of people give hope for a better future. Let us have those discussions and discoveries together.

Editor: Sasha Dessy, PhD
Interior and Cover Design: Chris Molé

Library of Congress Control Number: 2025917264

ISBN: 979-8-9986128-0-0 (paperback)
ISBN: 979-8-9986128-1-7 (ebook)
ISBN: 979-8-9986128-2-4 (audiobook)

To Jenna and Kerry.
Where I continue to learn
the most important lessons in life.
You enable a higher version of me.

Contents

Preface   vii

Introduction   ix

Chapter 1:   Dare to Evolve   1

Chapter 2:   Soil Regeneration   11

Chapter 3:   Clean Water   21

Chapter 4:   Restore Climate   33

Chapter 5:   Peace: Our Most Important Evolution   41

Chapter 6:   Holistic Health   55

Chapter 7:   Love and Compassion   69

Chapter 8:   We Are One   75

Chapter 9:   Education   85

Chapter 10:   Resonance   95

Chapter 11:   Regenerative Buildings   101

Chapter 12:   Clean Transportation   107

Chapter 13:   Energy   119

Chapter 14:   Zero Waste   127

Chapter 15:   Reimagine Economy   135

Afterword   145

Appendix One: Resources   147

Appendix Two: Statistics to Investigate   152

Appendix Three: Diversity   157

References: Key Names and Terminology   160

Acknowledgments   165

About the Author   169

"Our life is what our thoughts make it."

~ MARCUS AURELIUS

Preface

This is an invitation to embark on a journey—not to discover something new, but to remember what's always been within. A voyage of oneness, compassion, and resonance—not as lofty ideals, but as living energies already embodied. This book is a call to return to our true nature: congruent, whole, and deeply connected to all that surrounds us.

The intuition of unity reminds us we were never separate. The wind, the sea, the trees, each other—we breathe together in one great rhythm. Compassion arises from this realization. Not as sentiment, but as a sacred responsibility—to see through the illusions that divide us and meet each other in truth.

Resonance comes alive when our actions match our inner knowing. When we move in harmony with life's symmetry and action, and let integrity—not fear—guide our choices.

This book is not here to tell you what to think. It's a compass. A mirror. A remembering. Of the wholeness, the clarity, the quiet wisdom that has always been yours.

In a world spinning with chaos, we are not being asked to fix it all. Each of us is being invited to become the change—gently, boldly, bravely. Become the message when you dare to live from truth. Surrender the need to know, and trust that the answer lives in your being.

May these pages open something in you. May you walk your path with courage. May your resonance call others home.

Live truth—and keep questioning it. Live kindness. Be willing. Be real. Be whole. Be able.

Introduction

In a time when we are experiencing so many challenges that seem to get all the press, it is vital that we also are exposed to working sustainable solutions across a variety of categories. Physics is now clarifying our existence and the nature of our reality. It is becoming clearer that everything comes from an energy that is difficult to explain and understand. The conclusions are that there is an energy which enables the planet and all existence on it—with each tree being enabled in much the same way that a human is, only with different boundaries. Humans are able to affect change. It is time for us to seek our greater potential. We can use these insights to shift our thinking.

Our familiar world is changing beneath our feet. Our long-standing systems for energy, food, water, and peace are all under strain. The effects of extractive industries that have separated us from the natural cycles of life are reflected in climate change, environmental deterioration, and escalating social conflicts. However, these challenges also present a significant opportunity—to evolve.

More than a call to action, *Dare to Evolve* is an invitation to reconsider how we construct, live within, and interact with the world. This book is a journey toward a mindset of regeneration, connection, and internal reflection, not a manual on sustainability as a far-off idea. It is about the silent revolution that starts inside each of us.

We are living in a time of deep uncertainty where it is difficult to discern truth. This requires that we use our intuition—the deep knowing that everything is interrelated. Everything we do has an impact, just as everything around us affects us. We are all in this together, regardless of our beliefs, and it is time to nurture a support system to challenge our assumptions to find resolutions that serve everyone.

This process of looking at something and then questioning our belief about it is often frustrating. Any time we are in the middle of learning something new we experience that uncomfortable space that often keeps us from moving forward. We would rather just make a decision to accept or deny something without truly resolving it in our mind. How do we move ourselves into the resilience of knowing something new and then have the bravery to be open to the possibility that the truth we decided on may need to be questioned again. The longer we tolerate the awkward feeling in that learning space the more we evolve the human species. It happens one courageous person at a time.

My father had two expressions that taught me that true change begins by looking inward for solutions. Whenever I would get annoyed about something in the world, he would say: "Sounds like a personal problem to me." Other times when I would escalate to anger and carry on, he would say: "You know you have the same clothes to get glad in." His words, though simple, carried a profound truth: our power lies in how we choose to respond to the world, not react to it. My spouse Kerry also reminds me of this.

Stories of creatives, individuals, groups, and communities reclaiming traditional knowledge while developing new technologies can be found across these pages. Every chapter offers a glimpse of the solutions that are now available to us, from renewable energy initiatives that challenge the dominance of fossil fuels to regenerative agriculture that restores depleted soils. However, the remedies alone are insufficient; we must have the courage to change the way we think, reinterpret our wants, and foster connection with the Earth and each other.

This book's path reflects the cycles of nature, starting with awareness and progressing to inquiry, involvement, and introspection. The stories of farmers, scientists, spiritual leaders, and regular people who are accepting the challenge of evolution—not via war, but through creation—will speak to you. This is not a how-to book. Rather it is examples of sustainable solutions that show there are alternatives being used today. You are encouraged to support these organizations in their goals to empower solutions. Or, start your own.

To truly know myself and my place, I spend time in nature. Whether we are willing to change into a species that coexists peacefully with the planet that supports us is more important than whether we can bring the planet back into balance. While limited in scope, one chapter at a time, *Dare to Evolve* opens the door to possibility rather than providing a single answer. This will continue to be a challenge as each new generation must be enabled to see the possibilities beyond our typical egocentric paradigm. There are already many sustainable solutions in progress, some of which you will find in these pages. May these examples inspire you to join in and go further.

Whenever you find yourself asking: Why is this happening to me? Come into presence and ask: How is this occurring for me? Decide and move forward. Inquire again if needed.

Come into the moment. Be inquisitive rather than judgmental. Be intentional with your time and purpose. Investigate and study. Enjoy beautiful moments with others and in nature. Gather. Be open and flexible. Be curious to understand. Learn anew. Be willing to unlearn and relearn, for we are seldom right the first time. Be vibrant with a kind heart.

Let us begin with love.

DARE TO EVOLVE

"Do the best you can until you know better.
Then when you know better, do better."

~ Maya Angelou

CHAPTER 1

Dare to Evolve

In the landscape of transformation, true change begins within. How do we seek to align with the divine design of all that is? For most people, sustainable solutions are not a question of unfamiliarity—they are a challenge of shifting deeply ingrained mindsets. To embrace change, we must first come to terms with the discomfort it brings. To enable people and communities to coexist peacefully with the environment and one another, let's examine how cognitive dissonance, social influence, and emotional resonance can guide us through that discomfort. Which in turn, can move us toward a deeper awareness of and a collective shift toward sustainability. We must shift to get back in touch with the world, and live in a way that respects both our duty and its wisdom. Even then, we must continue to challenge our cognitive dissonance in order to find the best path. What are we willing to relearn to support more congruent solutions? It is a challenge to cross that bridge of questioning our beliefs.

Astronauts have often commented on how the first view of Earth from space changed their perspective creating the sense there are "neither borders, nor boundaries." Seeing the fragility of this planet puts into perspective that life is not about building an economy for exploitation but rather a collaboration for the health of all. While this is an experience the average person will not share, even viewing a picture of our planet from space can impart a sense of wonder. A beautiful marble in the vastness of space. When we allow it into our psyche and consider everything we experience when we look around, it becomes intuitive that we are living in an illusion. One that is manipulated to seem as though things are more important than relationships. Let us Dare to Evolve toward loving all that is. Dare to venture out, confront our currently held beliefs, and courageously consider different ideas. Evolve to see new possibilities and be open to adopting the alternative.

Survival is the goal of all life. We see this when we observe a plant sprouting out of a crack in the sidewalk or a tree growing around a boulder. Survival for humans has changed many times since living in the wild and protecting ourselves from tigers, lions, and other predators. We developed the ability to build shelters and grow crops to assure a larger number of survivors. With each step, human evolution has enabled population growth. We then continued to invent new ways to ensure our comfort and protection from the elements. While some of these were good for our species, others have created many of the problems we face today.

Humanity stands at a crossroads, faced with a choice to continue the *unsustainable* practices that have led to environmental, health, and social degradation or to embark on a new journey—a journey toward sustainable living, harmony, and wholeness. The need to evolve, to shift our thinking and our actions, is undeniable. Chaos is uncomfortable and precarious. However, it is often in times of pandemonium that we are motivated to seek better answers. This is how positive evolution can enable workable solutions.

Just like a hero or heroine at the beginning of a journey, we are being called to awaken, to recognize that the status quo no longer serves us. Our current systems—whether economic, agricultural, conflict resolution, sickness care, or social—are unsustainable. Nature herself has been sending us signals, asking us to listen and change course. The heroes and heroines of this journey are the everyday people who choose to see a truth, challenge the old paradigms, and step into the unknown with courage. Then do it again.

I was four when we moved to Idaho. We lived in the country. As an energetic and curious young boy, I was enthralled with the frogs in the gravel ponds behind our property. It was nature at its best with snakes, pheasants, ducks, and other creatures. Watching polliwogs grow and transform into frogs was exciting. Spending hours in that environment gave me an appreciation of how many things are interconnected by supporting not only themselves, but others also. To make money for the bubblegum machine, and an occasional candy bar, my cousin and I would walk the roads and pick up the bottles people had thrown out of their cars. We sold the bottles back for the deposit. During that time, while I was grateful for the money I made, I was also very puzzled by their behavior. How could people think it was ok to pollute such a divine system. Nature is so interconnected. I was so blessed to be raised in such a beautiful environment, rich with a diversity of plants and animals, and have the freedom to wander and be in awe of their interaction with each other.

Many years later, while living in an apartment building in the 1970s, I was introduced to the idea of sustainable solutions for the first time. Another couple mentioned the recycling centers that were being established in our city. They thought we should make it easier for tenants in the building to recycle by gathering items in bins at the apartment building, and then we could take a big load to the center. Not really being educated on the need for recycling, I had to first investigate and then decide if it was something I supported. That process helped me recall how I had once been so connected to nature instead of being so complacent. It was difficult to change my prioritization of work to accept that I could make time to take these bins, etc. to the city recycling site. After overcoming my cognitive dissonance and realigning my being with what I intuitively knew was right, we organized the bins and started doing weekly visits to the new recycling center. It took some adjusting of my desires, but it gave me a feeling of accomplishment and a sense of the potential for a better world. We later moved out of that building, but when visiting a friend who had moved into the same building, it was encouraging to find that the recycling system was all still in place. A few years later, the city started gathering recycling at the curb. Progress happens.

There have been occasions throughout my life when I found myself out of alignment with our divine natural architecture. In many cases, I was totally unaware that my actions were not in alignment with my being. I am so grateful when I have experiences that help me to reconnect to that early knowledge that everything is connected.

Many of us are caught between the world we know and the world we need to create. Every great journey begins with a challenge—an invitation to see the world differently. In this case, the challenge lies within our thinking. At the core of every meaningful change is cognitive dissonance—holding two opposing thoughts at the same time—the tension we experience when our actions don't align with our beliefs. Imagine using plastic bags out of convenience despite having serious concerns about the pollution that plastic causes. The clash between belief and action creates psychological unease. We may respond by justifying our behavior, but the courageous among us lean into the discomfort. We recognize that the friction is a signal, a guidepost, that something needs to shift. And this process is not just about avoiding discomfort—it's about evolving toward choices that better support the self, daring ourselves to change, and aligning our values with higher, more balanced solutions.

The propensity to look for evidence to support our already-held beliefs is known as confirmation bias, and it frequently keeps us from considering alternative viewpoints. It's simpler to hold onto our comforting beliefs than to question our worldview. This prejudice keeps us stuck in our ways of thinking, which makes it difficult to change.

But we have to get out of our comfort zone if we want to progress. We have to be open to exploring concepts that push our boundaries and cause us to reevaluate our presumptions. To truly evolve, we must be curious and open to learning things beyond what we know.

Because we are social creatures, others around us have a big impact on the decisions we make. It inspires us to adopt sustainable activities when we witness others doing so. Conversely, it can be more difficult for us to take environmentally friendly actions when people in our social circles disregard environmental issues.

For civilization to truly advance, we must cultivate environments where sustainability is the rule rather than the exception. Social influence has the potential to be a very effective tool for good by inspiring people to make decisions that respect the environment and one another.

Not everything transforms at once. Change emerges from gradual exposure to novel approaches of doing and thinking. Our smaller actions, such as cutting back on plastic use, saving energy, and promoting regional food systems, add up to something bigger. They gather momentum over time.

The key is to embrace the small steps while keeping the larger vision in mind—each new step lays the foundation for more profound systemic shifts in behavior.

Data and facts alone rarely drive action. Emotional resonance—stories that touch our hearts—often moves us toward change more effectively. When we connect emotionally to the impact of unsustainable practices on the planet or future generations, our cognitive dissonance becomes harder to ignore. It's the difference between knowing something intellectually and feeling it deeply in your heart. This emotional empathy compels many people to align their choices with their values. This book includes numerous examples of such changes across a variety of categories. Some will speak to you, while others may not. It is my hope there will be something that will engage your desire to experience a feeling of congruence with the whole, that knowing from the intuitive self. Our involvement with solutions always makes a difference towards a better ecosphere. Whatever your interest challenge yourself to engage in a positive manner.

The shift from passive awareness to active change is a dynamic process, one that unfolds through several stages. Each step of the process moves us closer to living a life that is consistent with our values. Being aware is the first step. This is when we start to realize how our activities affect our environment. Awareness creates the space for change, whether it is in the form of recognizing the trash we produce and the impact it has or the effects of our energy usage. However, awareness on its own is insufficient; action is also essential.

As soon as we become conscious of these issues, we begin to inquire. Why do I still follow these routines? Is there a better way? This is a critical stage of change -- questioning the status quo. It challenges us to evaluate our actions and the systems in which we are involved. Evolution cannot occur without questioning. So, to spur your interest ask questions, seek and research for truth, get involved in areas of interest, be mindful when watching TV. Constrain your social media time. Limit areas where you turn off your mind. Instead of judgement embrace inquisitiveness.

Once our curiosity is sparked, we seek information. To find answers and gain a deeper understanding of the problems at hand, we look at the information and, by studying the patterns, turn it into knowledge. Knowledge equips us to make wise decisions, whether it is on regenerative agriculture, renewable energy, or lessening our carbon footprint.

Armed with new knowledge, we begin to experiment. It's the moment when we start putting what we've learned into practice. We might start small, like composting at home, using less water, or buying from companies that put sustainability first. The link between knowledge and action is participation in seeking an alternative.

The transformation begins with action. Research and testing are the moments when we start to match our actions to our moral principles. We begin to live change rather than just contemplate it. Every choice we make, like recycling, using renewable energy, or cutting back on consumption, becomes a declaration of our dedication to living in congruence.

Change is not a single event; it is a continual process of reflection and reinforcement. We consider the outcomes while we act. We then observe the effects these changes have on our surroundings and our own lives. This contemplation, paired with action strengthens our resolve and makes our new habits more ingrained. It also inspires us to keep developing and looking for fresh approaches to coexisting peacefully with the planet.

Change is uncomfortable, yet it is the most constant entity in the universe. We must be conscientious. Confronting the ways in which our actions fail to live up to our beliefs is not easy. It's difficult to move into the unknown and give up the comforts you know to pursue something bigger. However, it's essential. We must have the courage to shift our actions if we want to build a world in which all may flourish.

This process involves more than personal decision-making; it entails raising our collective awareness. It all comes down to learning to live with the discomfort that accompanies change and letting it lead us to a more peaceful, sustainable way of life. Have the curiosity and bravery to learn something, question, unlearn, and relearn with an unguarded, adaptable mind.

While I am encouraged by the things I have learned, I have also become aware of how much I still do not know. I recognize there is always the possibility that I am wrong about what I thought I knew, and therefore need to be open to unlearning and seeking anew. The blessing of a universe of possibilities.

It is a call to action to evolve. It is an encouragement to live a life that is respectful of the planet, ourselves, and one another. When we have the courage to change, we join a bigger movement that aims to achieve more than merely survival. As we are all interconnected, our choices about how to evolve contribute to the creation of a world that affects the health and happiness of the Earth and all of its inhabitants.

Visit your sovereign space within, that self-determining universe only you can rule, and enable your curiosity. Remember in awe the marvelous interrelation of everything that exists and how each piece supports not only itself but also willingly sustains something else.

Where are you in resonance with the gift you are here to bring? How are you going to encourage and share that brilliance in your life moving forward? Can you create with ingenuity for the greater good?

Let us move forward for the sake of the planet, the next generation, and the potential for a more peaceful world—not out of fear but out of love.

Never underestimate the power of your conditioning.

"The two most important days of your life are the day you were born and the day you find out why."
~ MARK TWAIN

How can we shift our daily actions and mindset to contemplate a change in our thinking?

"Upon this handful of soil,
our survival depends."

~ Sanskrit text, 1500 BC

CHAPTER 2

Soil Regeneration

Regeneration is a process that aims to renew or restore something to its vigorous, natural state. Beneath our feet, the Earth is alive and continually renews itself if we give it the chance. Regenerative agriculture is a technique that respects the cycles of nature and aims to regenerate the soil, restore ecosystems, and feed communities. Regenerative methods are rooted in ancient wisdom that is still highly relevant today. There are many advantages of regenerative agriculture, ranging from the health of our planet to the quality of our food.

We come from nature; we return to nature. Worms in a compost pile seem to come out of nowhere. A mother takes nutrients from Earth to pass to the baby she is carrying for it to develop into the miracle of another human. Each person stays alive by taking in these same nutrients. When these nutrients are compromised for any reason, we are all losing our highest potential. Regenerative agriculture ensures we will continue to get the necessary nutrients for a healthy future. When we make this realization, it becomes easier to evolve our thinking to seek out foods that are whole, natural and investigate their nutrition base. This leads to considering farmers markets with local growers that are practicing regeneration of the soil with organic non-chemical methods. In some locations there are also grocery co-ops that only carry organic foods. I am encouraged that there are now foods labeled "Regenerative Organic Certified."

Soil regeneration, beyond improving agriculture will assist in cleaning our air and water. Incorporating of a variety of plant species improves the soil's ability to operate as a carbon sink, removing carbon dioxide from the atmosphere and so improving air quality. Healthy soil can also filter and cleanse water more efficiently due to its improved structure and enhanced microbial activity. By lowering runoff, it lessens pollution and nutrient accumulation that eventually depletes oxygen. Improved soil structure leads to increased water infiltration and retention, which supports human and ecological health by replenishing groundwater sources and preserving constant water quality. Biodynamic agriculture, developed by Rudolf Steiner, also promotes a wholistic approach to enabling nature to interact in congruence with all. It promotes a holistic, ecological, and ethical approach to farming, gardening, food and nutrition. As such this approach aligns with other regenerative practices.

The importance of regenerative practices is evident when we spend more time in the natural world. Whenever I walk among the trees and abundant undergrowth near a creek here, the energy that comes from everything around me seems interdependent. Each supports not only itself but shares with all that is around it. The idea that nature operates in interconnected systems lies at the core of regenerative agriculture. Every activity has a knock-on influence, affecting not only the soil but also the air, water, and food that are necessary for life.

∼

There are numerous advantages to regenerative practices:

Food: Food produced in wholesome, regenerative systems is more nutrient dense, which is advantageous to consumers. Put simply crops that grow in healthy soils produce healthier people. Communities, in turn are nourished by this cycle of nurturing both the soil and people.

Soil: Packed with bacteria, fungus, and other microorganisms that support a vibrant ecosystem, soil is a living thing. Holistic grazing, cover crops, and no-till farming are examples of regenerative techniques that enrich the soil rather than deplete it. Each year, the regenerative practices further increase the nutrients in the soil. Soil is one of nature's best resources for storing carbon since it becomes more balanced with time, holds water better, and stores more carbon.

Climate: Regenerative agriculture can be an effective means of mitigating the effects of climate change. In healthy soil, carbon dioxide from the atmosphere is absorbed and safely stored underground. Thus, regenerative agriculture aids in undoing the harm caused by industrial agricultural methods that have diminished the capacity of the Earth to absorb carbon dioxide.

Regenerative agriculture is predicated on the idea that nature's systems are flawless in and of themselves. After all, nature (where it has not been altered by humans) has been working to provide healthy, evolving outcomes since the beginning. Nature routinely supports higher potentials. Otherwise, none of us or any of the living Earth would be here. Nature's resilience is obvious when we consider the amount of unnatural chemicals, and toxins humans have unleashed on it, and yet it continues to recover and thrive.

Conventional farming practices, which mostly rely on monoculture crops and chemical inputs, upset the equilibrium and cause soil erosion, water scarcity, and biodiversity loss. However, by recognizing the interdependence of the soil, air, and water, regenerative agriculture operates in harmony with the natural world. Regenerative farming provides a route not only to sustainable living but also to regenerative living by emphasizing methods that restore rather than extract.

Growing up in an agricultural community in the 1950s gave me an appreciation for how farming is both frustratingly hard work and equally satisfying with the result of good, healthy crops. My father, after 28 years in the oil fields, moved our family to Idaho near my mother's parents. He started a water well drilling business and then also homesteaded 360 acres. We cleared the sagebrush, drilled a water well, and farmed it for 10+ years. It was interesting to experience the shifts in the farming community from small, locally owned farms that used minimal additives to a big AG model using pesticides and herbicides. The promises of easier bug and weed control, along with higher crop yields, were the major appeal of the new system. Farmer's use of these chemicals has triggered our soil to lose its ability to maintain the nutrients necessary for healthy crops – because the soil dies.

Where chemicals are consistently used crop yield declines. This is still the main model for agriculture in the United States. However, the number of chronic illnesses linked to chemical use increased dramatically as a result of relying on chemicals for farming. Cancer rates skyrocketed, and many of my own family friends were experiencing this by the late 1960s. Additionally, processing of food from these chemical-laden crops now includes added dyes and other toxic ingredients, resulting in food that has lost almost all of its nutrient value. This issue seems to be the worst in the United States. My hope is that we can dare to evolve to a point where regenerative agriculture is the predominant paradigm.

Soil regeneration is more than just an ideal; farmers and innovators throughout the world are proving it to be a workable, realistic solution that is currently in use.

FARMS AND RANCHES

The Biggest Little Farm: This film about Apricot Lane Farms in California turning deteriorated land into a vibrant, regenerative environment, making it a symbol of hope. Through the adoption of permaculture principles, livestock rotation, and an embrace of biodiversity, the farm demonstrates how ecosystems may be revitalized when human intention is in harmony with the natural order.

Singing Frogs Farm: This no-till, extremely diverse farm in California is now regarded as a model for regenerative agriculture. The farm delivers an abundant output, improves soil health, lowers erosion, sequesters carbon, and safeguards water resources by doing away with tillage. It also serves as an example of how a small local farm can produce healthy foods and, at the same time, enable an economic impact that is among the highest profits per acre.

Oak Mountain Farm: A regenerative farm in Oregon that combines pasture management with holistic grazing. Oak Mountain Farm rehabilitates the land, improving soil health and biodiversity by utilizing natural processes and rotating cattle.

Polyface Farms: Joel Salatin's Polyface Farms use regenerative concepts and rotational grazing to establish a harmonious environment that fosters cooperation among soil, plants, and animals. This symbiosis produces a sustainable food system, lowers waste, and improves soil fertility.

Parker Pastures: This Colorado based regenerative ranch builds soil health, sequesters carbon, and promotes biodiversity via holistic grazing. Their model shows how regenerative livestock techniques can improve the productivity of the land by interacting harmoniously with the natural world.

Tabula Rasa Farms: This farm embodies the essence of regenerative agriculture, merging ethical animal husbandry with sustainable land stewardship. Their approach prioritizes soil restoration, biodiversity, and holistic land management to create a self-sustaining ecosystem. By growing pasture-raised livestock without antibiotics or hormones and integrating rotational grazing, the farm enhances soil health while producing nutrient-dense food. More than just a farm, Tabula Rasa serves as a model for how agriculture can regenerate the environment, nourish communities, and foster deeper connections between people and their food. Through their work, they demonstrate that farming, when done with care and intention, can be a force for ecological renewal and food security.

POLICY / EDUCATION

Farmer's Footprint—Zach Bush MD: This program attempts to enhance human health and restore soil health. Dr. Bush highlights the strong links between soil quality and chronic disease. He promotes mending the land by lowering chemical inputs and adopting regenerative solutions as a means of healing ourselves. This is a great example of daring to evolve beyond Dr. Bush's training to a larger awareness with action toward what integrates a higher purpose. His insights are profound as well as inspiring and motivating.

The Need to Grow **Documentary**: This film looks at cutting-edge farming techniques that could heal the environment and our food systems. The Need to Grow demonstrates how regenerative methods can help combat climate change and maintain food security in the future.

Vesper Meadow: This Oregon-based education initiative uses regenerative techniques to enable native plant restoration. They have engaged people from ages six to ninety-one in workshops and mentoring. Results are tracked with science-based research to re-enable nature at its best. They focus on education plus results.

Regeneration International: An international organization that advocates for the use of regenerative agriculture as a vital instrument in combating climate change. Regeneration International links farmers, scientists, and policymakers to promote regenerative techniques through research, teaching, and advocacy. All of these efforts support a cleaner environment as well as empowering better local economies.

Understanding AG: This group works with farmers to apply regenerative techniques that improve crop yields, strengthen soil health, and foster climate resilience. Their work is based on scientific principles and aims to provide farmers with the necessary resources to thrive in a regenerative system.

Kiss the Ground: This nonprofit organization is essential in bringing attention to the significance of soil health. Through advocacy and education, Kiss the Ground teaches individuals that the ground beneath our feet holds the answer to healing our planet.

Wild Minds Community: The Wild Minds Community is committed to building a future in which regenerative farming and off-grid living coexist to benefit both people and the environment. Their strategy, which is based on the ideas of ecological balance and self-sufficiency, places a high priority on reclaiming damaged land using sustainable techniques including agroforestry, permaculture, and holistic land management.

Ballymaloe Cookery School: In County Cork, Ireland, the Ballymaloe Cookery School promotes the farm-to-table concept by fusing sustainable farming methods with culinary instruction. Located on a 100-acre organic farm, the school stresses the value of knowing the origins and production processes of food. Every facet of the food cycle is taught to students, from cultivating and gathering organic produce to cooking meals that highlight local and seasonal ingredients.

Flora Farms: This farm in Mexico is proof of the effectiveness of farm-to-table, sustainable living. This 25-acre organic farm, tucked away in the Sierra de la Laguna Mountains' foothills, grows seasonal produce without the use of genetically engineered seeds or artificial pesticides. In addition to producing food, Flora Farms cultivates a whole community focused on conscious living, artisanal crafts, and regenerative farming. Their on-site cottages, spa, and workshops immerse guests in a sustainable and natural lifestyle, while their field kitchen prepares meals straight from the farm. Flora Farms serves as a vibrant example of community-driven food systems and responsible land stewardship by combining organic farming, hospitality, and education.

Babylonstoren: A historic Cape Dutch farm In the Drakenstein Valley of South Africa, Babylonstoren serves as a sentient illustration of both farm-to-table living and regenerative agriculture. The farm, which spans more than 200 hectares, combines ecological sustainability with organic food production. Its carefully planned garden provides fresh produce for its well-known restaurants. Babylonstoren prioritizes biodiversity, soil health, and closed-loop farming—where nothing is wasted—by using natural growing techniques. In order to strengthen their bond with the land, visitors can participate in practical activities like winemaking, beekeeping, and harvesting. In addition to protecting the area's agricultural legacy, Babylonstoren provides a model for sustainable food systems around the globe by fusing innovation and tradition.

William Holden Wildlife Foundation (WHWF): To counteract land degradation brought on by chemical-intensive agriculture, the WHWF in Kenya is actively involved in education about permaculture farming and soil restoration. Understanding that excessive use of pesticides and fertilizers reduces soil fertility and biodiversity, WHWF trains subsistence farmers in sustainable methods to revitalize their fields. With the help of the Annenberg Grant, the foundation has established soil regeneration initiatives in five different areas, teaching herding communities how to restore important grasslands for their animals. Under the direction of Katie Mclean and her skilled staff, WHWF highlights the value of composting and natural farming methods, showing that with commitment even the most depleted soils can be restored to promote abundant farming.

SEEDS

A diverse bank of seeds is essential to regenerative agriculture. Adaptable crops are integral to the health of ecosystems because they can change with the environment.

Baker Creek Heirloom Seeds: This company, which specializes in rare and heirloom seeds, encourages biodiversity by providing farmers and gardeners with access to a broad variety of crops.

Seed Savers Exchange: By sharing and preserving heirloom seeds, this nonprofit contributes to the preservation of genetic diversity in our food chain. Seed Savers Exchange promotes the regenerative movement by equipping farmers and gardeners with the tools they need to develop resilient crops.

Rogue Valley Heritage Grain Project: An organization whose mission is to increase access to seeds of climate resilient, culturally significant food staples through grower participation and community education.

While there are many additional examples of regenerative agriculture, these show that the model is available and it works.

Regenerative agriculture is a deliberate choice to work with rather than against the Earth's natural rhythms. It is more than just farming. It's a practice that guarantees the well-being of future generations in addition to providing food for us today. Regenerative agriculture provides a blueprint for healing the land and ourselves by preserving biodiversity, improving soil health, and sequestering carbon.

When we dare to change, we can be mindful that every decision we make and every seed we sow has the potential to replenish or deplete. Regenerative agriculture creates systems of abundance, resilience, and hope by choosing to give back to the Earth as much as we take. Let us respect the knowledge of the Earth and the delightful interrelatedness it exhibits as we proceed, understanding that it is its renewal that renews us as well.

"Plant a tree every year."
~ Hope Jahren

Love the Earth, for it is us.

How can we shift our daily actions and perspectives to consider sustainable solutions for soil regeneration?

"Water is life, and clean water means health."

~ Audrey Hepburn

CHAPTER 3

Clean Water

L ife's vital force is water. It links, nourishes, and maintains all living things. Nothing can flourish without it. However, access to clean water—a fundamental human right—is under threat in the world in which we live. Pollution, over-extraction, and climate change have contaminated many of our vital water sources. Daring to evolve means acknowledging water as a living being deserving of respect and preservation rather than merely as a resource. Here we look at ways to heal our contaminated waters and establish a regenerative connection with this precious element.

Water is so entwined with our environment that a lack of clean, healthy water affects every phase of the succession. Every stage of ecological progression is impacted by a shortage of clean, safe water since water is so interwoven with our surroundings. For example, early colonizing plants that anchor the soil may not take root in a polluted marsh, delaying the arrival of insects, birds, and finally trees. The regenerative process comes to a complete stop. Life cannot build up layers of richness without clean water.

CLEAN WATER AS A FUNDAMENTAL RIGHT

Life itself is found in water. It is not a luxury to have access to clean water, nor should be considered one. Clean water is necessary for every person on the globe to be well and happy. There are cascading impacts when people lack access to clean water: food becomes more difficult to grow, diseases multiply, and entire ecosystems fail. Our disconnection from the Earth and its natural processes is reflected in the global water catastrophe we are currently facing. Restoring clean water means healing the earth and ourselves by restoring balance.

Millions of people throughout the world fight every day to get access to safe water. Families may trek miles to gather water in areas where it is scarce or contaminated, and the water is often unhealthy to consume. Women and children bear this load disproportionately, which affects their capacity to work and go to school.

But exercising the inherent human right to water requires action. We have to face the fact that more than a billion people still do not have access to clean drinking water and that industrial pollution is continuing to poisoning our rivers, lakes, and seas. Restoring our water systems is about more than just survival; it's about building a society in which all people may prosper.

I grew up near the Snake River in Idaho. Our recreation on the river was water skiing. Although I was unaware of it at the time, the boat exhaust was contaminating the water. But water skiing was a personal blessing in terms of boosting my belief in my athletic ability. Hence the need for electric or hydrogen boats.

When tested, the water wells that my father drilled were frequently very pure and didn't require any kind of treatment. Today, the majority of water sources need to be treated or filtered to prevent health problems. Every nation on the earth should be obligated to provide access to clean water, and international cooperation and collaboration should be fostered to make this possible.

Charity: *Water—A Lifeline for Communities in Need*
One of the most influential organizations working to address the world's water crisis is Charity: Water. Their goal is to provide people in poor countries with access to clean, safe drinking water. However, their contributions have a much greater effect than merely building filtration systems or wells. They increase health outcomes, free up time for education, and lay the groundwork for economic growth by providing clean water.

The focus of Charity Water's initiatives is sustainability. To make sure clean water is a permanent resource rather than merely a band-aid fix, they collaborate with nearby towns and train leaders in water system maintenance. An essential component of water regeneration is this community involvement approach, which recognizes that access to clean water is a shared responsibility.

SeaHugger: *Healing Our Oceans One Shore at a Time*
There is a direct correlation between the condition of our freshwater systems and the health of our seas. A nonprofit organization called SeaHugger is committed to clearing plastic debris from beaches and coastal waters. They serve as a reminder that many of the contaminants that end up in our freshwater supplies are also present in our oceans, including plastic, microplastics, and poisons.

One of the most common contaminants, plastic, never really decomposes. Rather, it breaks up into minuscule particles and seeps into the food and water we consume. To address this issue, SeaHugger plans beach cleanups, promotes reduced use of plastics, and highlights eco-friendly substitutes. Their efforts highlight a crucial reality: eliminating pollution at its source rather than merely treating its consequences later is the key to restoring clean water.

4Ocean is a global cleanup initiative dedicated to removing plastic waste from oceans and coastlines while promoting sustainable solutions to the world's water pollution crisis. Through the sale of bracelets and other eco-friendly products made from recycled materials, 4ocean funds professional cleanup operations in some of the most polluted waterways. Their efforts extend beyond waste removal, as they also focus on community education, advocacy for reducing single-use plastics, and supporting sustainable fishing practices. By employing local workers and utilizing innovative cleanup technologies, 4ocean has removed millions of pounds of trash from the ocean, demonstrating the power of consumer-driven environmental action.

UpTerra: *Water Solutions* By improving water quality to benefit the health of crops and livestock, UpTerra is transforming the agricultural industry. Their technology benefits soil, plants, and animals by converting regular irrigation water into a more hydrated and bioavailable form.

The UpTerra System comprises three key components:

1. Flow Device: This apparatus arranges water into an optimal state by simulating vortexing and turbulence, two natural water processes. Cells can more easily absorb this structured water, resulting in better hydration.

2. Electronic Coils: Similar to how musical vibrations promote plant development, electronic coils imprint the structured water with beneficial absorption. By improving the health of plants, animals, and soil, this method lessens the need for chemical inputs.

3. TerraNet™: Soil nutrients and biostimulants are among the more than 150 digital amendments and inputs that UpTerra has created in its library. Low radio frequencies are used to deliver these to fields, focusing on certain regions to enhance soil nutrients and plant health or reduce pests.

UpTerra provides a comprehensive approach to agriculture by combining these elements, which lowers water and chemical use while fostering healthier ecosystems. This method improves the general health of our environment and restores natural water cycles in addition to increasing farm productivity.

ECOsmarte: *Chemical-Free Filtration for a Healthy Future* ECOsmarte uses natural processes instead of harsh chemicals to filter water, providing a technologically advanced answer to the problem of water filtration. Their systems clean water by using ionization and oxygen, offering a safe and environmentally acceptable substitute for conventional techniques that frequently employ chlorine or other harmful chemicals.

Chemical-free filtration safeguards natural ecosystems, which are frequently impacted by chemical runoff, in addition to public health. ECOsmarte's strategy envisions a regenerative future where we may enjoy clean water without compromising environmental health.

Clean Water Action: *Promoting Environmental Justice* A well-known advocacy organization, Clean Water Action works to preserve water resources by promoting environmental justice and changing policies. Through their efforts, more people have access to clean water, especially marginalized groups who are disproportionately impacted by water pollution.

Their method emphasizes the necessity of systemic change, which is another crucial component of water regeneration. Treating the symptoms of water contamination is insufficient; we also need to address the underlying causes of water pollution, which might range from antiquated water infrastructure to ongoing industrial activities. Clean Water Action pushes for investments in clean water technology that safeguard ecosystems and communities equally, as well as for stricter laws on industries that pollute.

The Water Project: *A Lifeline for Sub-Saharan Africa* Millions of people in sub-Saharan Africa face water scarcity on a daily basis. In order to provide wells, rainwater collection systems, and filtration technologies that guarantee year-round access to clean water, The Water Project collaborates with nearby communities to develop sustainable water infrastructure.

Their strategy is essentially regenerative because it emphasizes giving communities the capacity to manage their own resources in addition to supplying water. The Water Project helps ensure that access to clean water is more than just a temporary fix in these communities by developing a sense of ownership and educating local leaders.

Save The California Delta: *Protecting a Critical Ecosystem* Large stretches of agricultural land are irrigated by the California Delta. As the largest estuary on the west coasts of North and South America, the California Delta supplies fresh water to millions of people. Nevertheless, mismanagement and contamination pose a continual threat to the Delta. Save the California Delta Alliance is a group committed to protecting the environment and using sustainable water management techniques in order to restore this important ecosystem.

The Delta serves as a reminder that pure water is an essential component of a complex ecosystem that supports biodiversity and human life, not just a resource to be used. Save the California Delta Alliance promotes laws that safeguard the delicate equilibrium of water use, making sure that the interests of stakeholders in the urban, agricultural, and environmental domains are taken into equal consideration.

The Freshwater Trust: *Safeguarding and Restoring Waterways* The Freshwater Trust is committed to using creative, data-driven solutions to protect and restore freshwater ecosystems. In order to enhance the quality and quantity of fresh water, their on-the-ground initiatives concentrate on rehabilitating rivers, streams, and watersheds. This organization improves aquatic habitats and lowers pollution by modifying river channels, replanting native plants along waterways, and using sustainable agricultural methods. To ensure restoration operations are successful and efficient, the group also uses cutting-edge technology to pinpoint locations that would be benefit the most.

The Freshwater Trust exemplifies how cooperative, science-based strategies can lead the way to a sustainable future for our essential freshwater resources. Their work shows that we can achieve change through collaborations with communities, governments, and businesses.

Dig Deep: *Expanding Access to Clean Running Water* DigDeep is a nonprofit human rights group that works to guarantee all Americans have access to running, clean water. DigDeep carries out community-led projects to solve the serious issue of over 2.2 million Americans lacking access to basic water and sanitation services. Their projects include the Appalachia Water Project, which serves communities in West Virginia and Kentucky; the Navajo Water Project, which provides hot and cold running water to families on the Navajo Nation in New Mexico, Arizona, and Utah; and the Colonias Water Project, which targets underserved areas along the Texas-Mexico border.

DigDeep is an example of a comprehensive strategy to address water poverty in America. It makes investments in research, activism, and workforce development in addition to developing infrastructure to permanently narrow the water access gap.

Water.org: *Helping Communities Access Clean Water*
Water.org is changing lives by offering long-term solutions for clean water access in underprivileged communities. They enable communities to obtain small, affordable loans for rainwater harvesting systems, home water connections, and sanitation upgrades. They created their own financing program called the WaterCredit initiative to fund these loans. Water.org disrupts the cycle of water insecurity by empowering communities to manage their own water solutions, cutting down on time spent fetching water and enhancing general well-being and financial stability. Their strategy ensures that clean water becomes a long-lasting resource for enhanced quality of life by fostering more resilience.

Water For People Water for People is committed to giving communities all around the world long-term access to clean water and sanitary facilities. Their strategy, called Everyone Forever, focuses on collaborating with businesses, communities, and local governments to create long-lasting, resilient water infrastructure. In order to guarantee that water access is sustained long after initial projects are finished, Water For People makes investments in infrastructure, trains local leaders, and encourages hygiene education. Through dependable, self-sustaining water solutions their work not only enhances health outcomes but also gives communities the tools they need to prosper socially and economically.

Water for Good With an emphasis on long-term effects rather than short-term respite, Water for Good is dedicated to offering sustainable clean water solutions to rural people in need. They encourage communities to take charge of their water systems by combining safe water access with sanitation and hygiene education through their Vision of a Healthy Village concept. Water for Good focuses on preserving clean water sources for future generations by collaborating with local authorities and educating families about healthy habits. By providing better access to life's most vital resource, their work not only promotes resilience but also enhances health, empowering communities to end the cycle of poverty.

Erin Brokovich Report Renowned for her environmental activism, Erin Brockovich is drawing attention to the urgent problems associated with water contamination in the US. She addresses the troubling amount of hexavalent chromium (chromium-6) in the tap water of more than 260 million Americans in all 50 states in her book The Brockovich Report. The federal government still does not control this substance, which is notoriously linked to the Hinkley, California case. The national limit for total chromium is still set at 100 parts per billion, which many experts believe is insufficient for protecting human health. Brockovich highlights a serious weakness in public health protections by pointing out that, in spite of the acknowledged hazards, regulatory actions have not changed to address the pervasive contamination.

WATER AS SACRED, WATER AS LIFE

We have lost the sacredness of water in our haste to expand, grow, and extract. If we are to move toward a regenerative future, we must remember water is a lifeline that connects all living things; it is not a commodity. Restoring clean water also means restoring life itself.

Whether through technology, legislative reform, or community engagement, the organizations and programs described here offer compelling examples of how we may regenerate our dirty water systems. They serve as a reminder that in addition to fighting for our right to access clean water, we also need to respect it as a precious resource that is essential to life.

Wherever you are, communicate with your legislators and promote the right to clean water for every person as well as every farm and waterway.

We have to face the fact that water is a finite resource if we are to evolve. It is valuable, delicate, and worthy of our defense. By renewing water we are establishing a new way of life that honors the interdependence of all species on Earth rather than merely repairing a malfunctioning system.

"Everyone deserves to have clean water."

~ NYJAH HUSTON

How can we shift our daily actions and perspectives to reflect on sustainable solutions for clean water?

CHAPTER 4

Restore Climate

"The Earth is what we all have in common."

~ WENDELL BERRY

Restoring the climate is a spiritual as well as a technological undertaking. It challenges us to stay mindful of
our kinship with the planet, respect its cycles, and develop a
deeper bond with nature. Perceiving our planet as something
to control instead of to coexist with—have contributed to
the climate concerns. Restoring ourselves to collaboration
with instead of separate from is the first step toward restoring the climate.

In the 1950s, when my family traveled to see my aunt in
Los Angeles, we witnessed the results of our excessive reliance on fossil fuels. There was a distinct difference from the
high air quality of our home in Idaho. Though it wasn't the
main attraction, the smog of foul-smelling air that pervaded
Anaheim when my father took me to Disneyland was
nonetheless extremely apparent. Years later, it was obvious
there was a lot of air pollution where we lived—in Southern
California in the late 1960s and Northern California from
the 1970s until mid-2017. Although there has been some
improvement, there are still bad-air days that are unaccept-
able for the residents' health and well-being.

In today's world, it is widely assumed that humans are
highly responsible for our climate crisis. While it is clear
there has been a shift in the climate, I also believe some
of this is the Earth's natural cycles that are in response

to universal influences from space. The shifting of the magnetic north pole may also be affecting our climate. The magnetic north pole has been rapidly changing over the last forty years, from its historical location in northern Canada towards Siberia. Because the movement affects everything from smartphone apps to airline routes and military navigation, experts are updating navigational systems more regularly as a result of the migration's rapid pace, which has averaged around 50 kilometers—about 31 miles —annually since the 1990s. Although this phenomenon is a normal aspect of Earth's geomagnetic behavior, scientists are examining if the shift is occurring more quickly because of alterations in the mechanics of the Earth's core or the distribution of glacier melt brought on by climate change. The changing magnetic pole emphasizes the interdependence of Earth systems and the necessity of adaptive technologies and international collaboration in monitoring planetary change, even if it is not directly driven by climate change. Additionally, continental drift, and earthquakes affecting parts of the earth could also be contributing to climate change.

That said, we can also recognize that the use of fossil fuels at the levels seen over the last 100+ years by humans has also contributed to our climate issues. I don't believe that we can return to a state where the climate is in balance just by humans responding in the best ways, they discover to mitigate pollution. It will help, but not totally restore the climate. We are going to have to learn new strategies to respond to the challenges we are experiencing with severe weather patterns, more intense and frequent fires, and the melting of glaciers, to give a few examples.

There are times when each of us finds ourselves in a balanced state with everything around us. These moments seem magical and remind me of how everything is interconnected and, simultaneously, how rare it is that I allow that realization to enter my consciousness. The energy seems to flow with its own knowing. When I try to make it happen, I understand the frustration of Luke Skywalker when Yoda tells him there is only do or not do. It only happens when I allow it, not when I try. Allowing brings a mysticism.

UN Global Compact: *The Call for Global Responsibility*
Restoring the climate requires a global response. The UN Global Compact is one such initiative aimed at mobilizing the power of businesses, governments, and civil society. This voluntary agreement calls for companies worldwide to align their strategies with universally accepted principles related to human rights, labor, the environment, and anti-corruption. Central to this effort is the commitment to sustainability.

Governments and activists cannot facilitate their contributions to climate change on their own. Businesses need to be involved because they consume significant resources and are major contributors to pollution. The UN Global Compact encourages companies to embrace sustainability as a core value. This can allow sustainability to guide all of their actions, rather than merely functioning as an afterthought. With the help of this compact, the business community is beginning to understand that it is a component of Earth's living system rather than a separate entity.

The Global Interdependence Coalition: *Seeing the Web of Life* According to the Global Interdependence Coalition we must first recognize our interconnectedness before we can restore the environment. All earthly systems, whether created by humans or not, are interdependent. Damage to one is damage to all. In an effort to change the discourse surrounding climate action, this coalition brings together activists, economists, environmentalists, and thought leaders. It's important to understand the intricately interwoven processes that make up our world, not merely to cut emissions.

For us to advance, we need to stop treating climate restoration as a collection of discrete acts and instead view it as a comprehensive, regenerative process. The Global Interdependence Coalition serves as a reminder that cooperation and an understanding of our place in the greater web of life are key to finding solutions to the climate catastrophe.

Aclima: *Data-Driven Restoration* To repair the climate, we must first identify the areas that have sustained the most harm and require immediate attention. Aclima offers environmental intelligence by using sensor technology to map air quality, carbon emissions, and pollution in real time. Communities, companies, and governments can then use this data to help them decide where to focus their efforts on climate restoration.

The advancement of climate action depends on technologies such as Aclima's. It breaks down the enormous problem of climate restoration into quantifiable, actionable steps, providing a sense of focus and clarity. Aclima assists us in navigating the route to regeneration by shedding light on the invisible—the carbon we emit, and the air we breathe.

The Intergovernmental Panel on Climate Change (IPCC): *Guiding Global Policy* Leading the field in climate science, the Intergovernmental Panel on Climate Change (IPCC) offers policymakers thorough scientific evaluations that serve as the foundation for international climate policy. Their studies offer a sobering reminder of the need for climate restoration, stressing the negative effects of inactivity and suggesting a path forward for our transition to a sustainable future.

The IPCC's research shows that climate restoration is not only feasible but also essential. They support systemic change, which includes cutting emissions, switching to renewable energy sources, and safeguarding wetlands and forests, that act as natural carbon sinks. Mitigating the damage is insufficient; we also need to rebuild the Earth's life-sustaining mechanisms.

American Forest Foundation: *The Power of Trees*
Nature provides some of the most potent instruments for restoring the climate, with forests being among the most successful. With an emphasis on replanting and sustainable forest management, the American Forest Foundation seeks to protect and restore forests throughout the country. Because they function as carbon sinks, removing carbon dioxide from the atmosphere and storing it in the soil, forests are essential to the health of the climate.

The American Forest Foundation is helping reverse of some of the harm caused by decades of deforestation and degradation by restoring forests. Their effort serves as a reminder that sometimes reviving the climate doesn't require new technology, but rather a return to the wisdom of nature.

Fridays for Future: *Youth at the Forefront of Change*
Greta Thunberg, a climate activist, started Fridays for

Future, a global youth-led campaign advocating for immediate climate action. This campaign is evidence of the growing influence of youth, who will bear the brunt of today's climate decisions. Their message is straightforward yet impactful: the era of gradual change is over. The climate emergency necessitates swift, decisive action.

The core of the climate movement is represented by the young people spearheading Fridays for Future. They lack the anxiety and complacency that can come with getting older and we lose our connection and alignment with nature. They have the audacity to change, forcing the outside world to match their urgency. They are a real-life example of what it means to pursue climate action with a greater conscience.

Extinction Rebellion: *Nonviolent Resistance for Climate Justice* Extinction Rebellion (XR) demands that governments respond immediately to confront the climate disaster through peaceful civil disobedience. This group draws attention to the seriousness of the climate catastrophe and the necessity of systemic change by upending business as usual. Even though their activities are contentious, their aim is to bring a sense of urgency to climate discussions that has long been lacking.

Extinction Rebellion urges truth-telling, which demands that businesses and governments be forthright about the seriousness of the climate issue. It also calls for the creation of a citizens' assembly so that the people can directly influence our future course. Because of XR's drastic approach to climate restoration, we are forced to consider revolution rather than just reform.

On Fire: The (Burning) Case for a Green New Deal In her book *On Fire,* Naomi Klein makes a strong case for the

Green New Deal, a complete set of laws intended to solve social inequality as well as the ecological problems. Beyond merely cutting emissions, the goal of the Green New Deal is to fairly transition society to a sustainable economy that benefits all people.

If we have the courage to change, the Green New Deal offers us an idea of what the future can hold. To assure that the shift to a low-carbon future is both just and inclusive, it is a call to restore not only the climate but also our communities and economies.

Sunrise Movement: *A Political Force for Change* Sunrise Movement is a youth-led political organization that supports the Green New Deal and other climate policies. They have been successfully raised awareness of climate change in the national political discourse of the United States through grassroots organizing.

The movement places a strong emphasis on the value of political participation and group action. Sunrise Movement is striving to make sure youth voices are heard in the political process since restoring the environment requires systemic change, not just individual efforts.

Dare to Restore: Mitigating harm or reducing the damage is not enough to restore the climate. Restoration involves having the audacity to imagine a different world in which people coexist peacefully with Earth's natural processes. It's about progressing toward regeneration and getting past exploitation. We are living in a pivotal moment in human history, and the decisions we make now will shape the planet for future generations. Our focus needs to be a healthy environment with healthy humans.

Our connection to the Earth is restored when we work to stabilize the climate. We rediscover the profound realization that we are a part of nature, not something distinct from it. We assume responsibility for the future and pledge to create a world in which all life can flourish when we have the courage to change. Working together, we can minimize human contributions to climate damage.

"Let us face it, there is no planet B."
~ EMMANUEL MACRON

How can we shift our daily actions and perspectives to think about sustainable solutions for climate restoration?

CHAPTER 5

Peace: Our Most Important Evolution

"See no stranger. See no enemy."
"You are a part of me I do not yet know."

~ VALARIE KAUR

Handling conflict by peaceful means is probably the best way to assure that sustainable solutions will enable our future.

Humanity's ability to accept peace is its greatest potential evolutionary achievement. Although there has been a lot of conflict in our history as a people, everyone has the capacity for peace. The 21st century has seen tremendous technological advancements, but global conflicts, inequality, and climate change continue to plague our societies. Yet the very instruments that have brought humanity perilously close to extinction also hold the key to the greatest possible innovation: a future free from warfare.

True peace is characterized by fairness, compassion, and a sense of oneness with all people, not only the absence of conflict. It's an intentional decision that calls for a deliberate change in the ways we interact, think, and lead. Now is the time to examine the path toward peace as the most significant evolutionary step, leading humanity toward a time when peace will always be the default state of affairs and violence will no longer be a viable option.

In my 20s, I experienced of the results of war first

hand. While on weekend flights as a medic in the Air Force reserve. I was responsible for taking care of wounded soldiers returning from Vietnam. My very first patient was a 19-year-old who was blinded and missing an arm and a leg. It changed my belief that violence was necessary to resolve conflict to believing that nothing we are fighting over is worth the brutality young men have to endure in war. Now we routinely witness news that more and more innocent civilians including children, are being killed in conflicts around the world. Peace is possible, and conflict resolution can work.

Revolutionary Love Project: *Recognize We Are One*
Understanding that we are one, as people, is the cornerstone of peace. It is a radical yet straightforward notion that all life is interrelated, interdependent, and has a common destiny. We start to recognize the pointlessness of fighting when we realize that the anguish and suffering of others resonate throughout our global community. Fundamentally, war stems from division—the idea that "they" are distinct from "us." However, the rationale for violence vanishes when we accept the reality of our common existence.

Recognizing that all people, regardless of their origins, ethnicity, or religion, have the same basic needs—to live with opportunity, security, and dignity—is the first step toward achieving peace. This realization changes not only the way we conduct international politics but also how we engage with people day-to-day.

Through the profound power of love, Valarie Kaur's Revolutionary Love Project provides an innovative method for promoting peace. The project reinterprets love as a force for justice, equity, and healing, based on her conviction that love can be an act of bravery and resistance. The framework is a useful tool for resolving conflicts, overcoming barriers, and fostering an empathetic culture by urging people to practice love for themselves, others, and opponents. I elaborate on this message in the chapter on love and compassion.

The principle of "seeing no stranger," which calls on us to perceive each individual as an integral part of ourselves, lies at the heart of the Revolutionary Love Project. This kind of thinking blurs the lines between "us versus them," promoting peace in divisive societies. This idea promotes communication and understanding in areas where fear or hatred could otherwise rule.

The project also highlights the need to love oneself, acknowledging that healing and inner strength are necessary for lasting action and peacemaking. By fostering resilience and preventing burnout, people are better able to stay rooted in their dedication to peace.

Furthermore, Kaur questions conventional ideas of warfare with her emphasis on loving opponents. Her perspective encourages behaviors that humanize enemies rather than reacting to hatred with hatred, creating the conditions required for restorative justice. Kaur often states, "There are no monsters; there are only those who are deeply wounded."

The Revolutionary Love Project provides a framework for addressing structural injustices and creating space for collective healing through its teachings, practices, and resources. Its focus on love as a revolutionary act has the power to inspire a more compassionate and peaceful society. Initiate peace with love!

Peace is a Choice

Peace is a decision, just like war. It is the result of deliberate effort and decision-making not something that happens by accident. To resolve conflict, every person, group, and country must consciously embrace peace as their guiding ideal. Making this choice takes courage, especially in a world where military force is frequently used to gauge authority and conflict is considered inevitable.

The resolution for peace starts on a personal level. The way we treat our neighbors, resolve disputes, and listen to those who have different opinions all contribute to the larger spectrum of world peace. Macroeconomically speaking, countries must decide between aggression and militarism or cooperation, diplomacy, and negotiation.

Instead of promoting exploitation, dominance, and violence, the movement toward peace aims to establish institutions and frameworks that encourage communication, equity, and justice. Realizing that every day we make decisions that either move us closer to or farther away from a peaceful world. It is our duty to enable wherever possible the evolution of peace.

The Deep Time Walk: *Seeing Our Place in History*

As a source of perspective and tranquility, the Deep Time Walk provides an important sense of planetary history. Participants experience the evolutionary unfolding of life on Earth as they walk 4.6 kilometers, with one meter signifying a million years. This contemplative practice cultivates awe and humility by firmly establishing the human tale in deep time. It dispels delusions of separation and serves as a reminder that all living things originate from the same extensive geological and biological arc. We all inherit the

Earth's story, which strengthens empathy among all species and generations. Walking through time turns into a journey toward quietude.

The Deep Time Walk serves as a powerful reminder of both the length of Earth's history and our fleeting existence on the planet. Walking through millions of years of Earth's history in real time helps us realize how transient human disputes really are. Despite their seeming enormity at the time, battles comprise but a small portion of the planet's lifespan.

Elders Action Network

A group of thoughtful seniors, the Elders Action Network (EAN) is dedicated to building a fair, compassionate, and sustainable future for all future generations. The network, which is based on the knowledge and expertise of its members, enables senior citizens to assume leadership positions and take an active part in environmental and social causes. EAN promotes a culture of peace and resilience through programs like intergenerational bridge-building, deep democracy discussions, and climate justice campaigning. Its Elder Circles and educational programs encourage elders to use their time, voice, and resources to help bridge divides and save the environment by giving forums for introspection, discussion, and concerted action. Elderhood has a crucial role in guiding humanity toward a more peaceful future, and the Elders Action Network reminds us that becoming older may be a source of strength.

Karen Harwell: *Never Been Here Before*

Through her work in trauma healing and conflict resolution, Karen Harwell serves as a reminder that each moment is unique and that we have never been here before. Nancy

Margulies film explores this remarkable statement, which sums up the spirit of evolution toward peace. We face never-before-seen difficulties as well as opportunities for change as we live in extraordinary times.

Harwell emphasizes narrative, attentive listening, and trauma recognition as crucial instruments for rapprochement in her analysis. For peace to truly establish itself in a world that has been severely damaged by war, healing must occur. Through accepting vulnerability, admitting past wrongs, and making a commitment to healing, people and communities can transcend the violent cycles that have shaped a great deal of human history.

Her efforts are a model for how we can engage with our own histories and trauma to create spaces for peace. Through collective healing, we create the conditions for lasting peace, built on understanding and empathy rather than force.

World BEYOND War: *A Global Citizens' Movement*
There is a worldwide grassroots movement dedicated to putting an end to all forms of warfare called World BEYOND War. This movement, which has 41 chapters in 30 nations, encourages common people to take a stand against war and works for a world without violence to settle disputes.

World BEYOND War focuses on the idea that since war is a human invention, it can be stopped. The movement supports disarmament, diplomacy, and shifting military spending to non-combative uses, including healthcare, education, and environmental restoration. It also emphasizes the significance of *Living Beyond War: A Citizens Guide*, a book that offers doable actions that anyone can take to help end conflict and demonstrate that everyone can play a part in bringing about peace.

Having worked in the original Beyond War movement in the 1980s, it is marvelous to see there are still people working on this around the world.

Breakthrough: Emerging New Thinking

Co-authored by Anatoly Gromyko and Martin Hellman, *Breakthrough: Emerging New Thinking* signaled a dramatic change in the Cold War mindset. Through their efforts, new perspectives on peace, security, and international relations were introduced. The authors maintained that international cooperation, mutual understanding, and the development of trust—rather than amassing armaments —are the true sources of security.

This new way of thinking paved the way for major arms reduction treaties and diplomatic achievements that helped defuse Cold War tensions. It serves as a reminder that achieving peace calls for creative problem-solving, a readiness to question established perception, and the guts to envision a future in which violence is never the solution.

It is regrettable that the politicians in NATO today do not uphold the terms of the agreements made during the reunification of Germany. It was agreed that NATO would not move eastward past the point at which Germany was reunited. Since then, NATO has expanded to include several of Russia's neighbors.

Conflict Resolution: *Education for a Peaceful Future*

Life will always involve conflict, but how we respond to it will either promote harmony or lead to bloodshed. The process by which disagreements are amicably resolved via dialogue, compromise, and understanding is known as conflict resolution. Programs like those at Portland State University's highlight how important it is to teach conflict resolution as a life skill.

Students pursuing degrees in conflict resolution are better equipped to ease tensions, and promote peace in a range of contexts, including interpersonal relationships and international diplomacy. We can ensure that disagreements are resolved amicably in the future by prioritizing conflict resolution education and avoiding the use of force.

Peace Corps: *A Catalyst for Global Understanding and Peace*
Since its establishment in 1961 by President John F. Kennedy, the Peace Corps has actively supported international peace initiatives by acting as a live example of cooperation and intercultural understanding. The Kennedy administration established it with the straightforward but significant goal of advancing global friendship and peace by sending volunteers to work on development projects overseas. These initiatives promote intercultural understanding while addressing issues of health, education, agriculture, and environmental sustainability.

A Community-Based Strategy for Peace
The Peace Corps is based on the idea that respect and personal relationships are the foundation of peace. Volunteers live and work among the residents and are immersed in the communities they assist, which are frequently in underserved and rural locations. They contribute to the development of long-lasting solutions to regional problems by exchanging information and expertise. In addition to empowering communities, this interpersonal interaction creates long-lasting bonds built on respect and trust.

Contributions to Global Sustainability
The Peace Corps prioritizes initiatives that foster long-term resilience, which is consistent with the ideas of sustainable

development. Volunteers frequently work on projects like clean water programs, regenerative agriculture, and climate adaption tactics that touch on the topics covered in this book. They assist communities in developing the capacity for sustainable living by offering creative yet contextually aware solutions.

Agents of Cultural Exchange

The cultural interchange that takes place is among the Peace Corps' most significant effects. Volunteers bring a deeper awareness of global issues and various lifestyles back to their home. In the same vein, host communities learn about different cultural viewpoints. The worldwide fabric of collaboration is strengthened, empathy is fostered, and stereotypes are demolished by this exchange.

A Modern Role in Peacebuilding

The purpose of the Peace Corps is more important than ever in the divisive world of today. The group advances the larger objective of a sustainable and peaceful planet by addressing the underlying causes of inequality and environmental degradation and bridging divides. The accounts of volunteers—ordinary people achieving incredible changes—provide hope and concrete illustrations of how compassion, teamwork, and a common goal may bring about peace.

The Peace Corps is a perfect example of how deliberate, modest acts may have a significant impact. Its volunteers exemplify that peace is a practice based on daily deeds of service and cooperation and not solely an ideal.

M. K Gandhi Institute for Nonviolence: *Gandhi's Legacy*

The M. K. Gandhi Institute for Nonviolence continues the tradition of nonviolent resistance, inspired by the ideals of

Mahatma Gandhi and Dr. Martin Luther King Jr. The institute offers peaceful protest and conflict resolution training
to both individuals and communities. Its goal is to show
that, in addition to being morally righteous, nonviolence is
a more practical means of bringing about enduring peace.

Nonviolence is a powerful tool for social change, as
evidenced by the civil rights, independence, and other significant nonviolent revolutions throughout history. The work
of the institute serves as a reminder that achieving peace
doesn't just happen; it takes bravery and active participation
to fight for justice without doing more harm.

International Cities of Peace: *A Global Commitment*
A global network of cities that have formally committed
to peacebuilding is known as the International Cities of
Peace initiative. These cities enact laws that support social
justice, lessen violence, and foster a peaceful society. The
effort demonstrates that peace can be established from the
ground up by operating locally.

Every City of Peace creates a special strategy for promoting peace that is adapted to the requirements and difficulties
of its locality. This movement serves as an example of how
systems that promote justice, equality, and the well-being
of all individuals are necessary for peace to exist.

Physicians for Social Responsibility: *The Health Impact
of War*
Due to the devastating impacts of war on human health,
Physicians for Social Responsibility (PSR) has long been at
the forefront of the movement to abolish nuclear weapons
and prevent war. In addition to the immediate brutality,
war has long-term effects on people's physical and mental

well-being. The destruction and pollution of infrastructure, and environment affects society in many unhealthy ways.

Peace, according to PSR, is a matter of public health. Healthcare experts argue that halting war is essential to protecting human health because conflict causes enormous amounts of illness, trauma, and suffering. PSR's work shows that supporting peace is not only a moral obligation but also a medical one.

Listen First Project

The Listen First Project advances peacebuilding by elevating the straightforward yet impactful act of listening. This campaign, which is based on the idea that true connection starts with compassion and curiosity, encourages people and communities to approach one another with open minds and hearts, especially when they are different. Listen First turns discussion into a means of mending conflict and rebuilding trust by encouraging dialogue rather than argument and understanding rather than condemnation. The act of genuinely hearing turns into a revolutionary step toward empathy, cooperation, and peace, whether it is between neighbors, political rivals, or complete strangers. The Listen First Project serves as a reminder that, in a society that is frequently characterized by noise and reactivity, finding tranquility can start with pausing, taking a deep breath, and having the guts to listen.

Books

Through his books The *Child on the Train* and *The Women of Ukraine*, photographer and narrator Christopher Briscoe provides a profoundly human perspective on the sorrow and resiliency resulting from conflict. Recommended reading to get a feel for the dismay of war.

Only Hope: A Survivor's Stories of the Holocaust by Felicia Bornstein Lubliner is a powerful and exquisite illustration of the human spirit's ability to endure oppression. She depicts the personal costs of living in a police state—a place where people's dignity is taken away, the truth is perilous, and terror reigns—with unwavering clarity. The brutality—the beatings, the silences, the betrayals—both public and private—is not something Lubliner hides. Her writing, however, has a subdued, obstinate elegance. She exposes the glimmer of humanity that endures despite gloom through characters that have emotions, pain, and the courage to dream. This story is about survivors rather than victims. About people who decide to trust in something greater despite all odds.

Only Hope's balance is what sets it apart. It is a celebration of inner strength, unity, and the little acts of defiance that add up to revolution, as much as it is a confrontation with violence within the mind. Lubliner's voice is forceful, empathetic, and accurate; it can capture terror without descending into hopelessness. This book serves as a reminder of the need for us to bear witness in an era when authoritarianism is on the verge of reemerging in many parts of the world. And why we should never give up.

Peter Russell examines in *The Global Brain*, now in its third edition, how an evolutionary leap in human consciousness can be triggered by the rise of the human population, which is expected to reach a peak of 11–12 billion. He suggests that mankind reflects the neurological complexity of a developing brain as more minds become connected through consciousness and technology. The collective network grows more perceptive, smarter, and able to incorporate other viewpoints with every additional individual. Once it reaches a critical mass, this global brain has the power to awaken a common consciousness that is based on collaboration rather than rivalry. According to Russell, peace is the natural manifestation of an evolved, unified species—a humanity that remembers its unity—rather than just the absence of strife. The urge to harm vanishes when we recognize ourselves as components of a greater whole, and is replaced by a profound empathy for all life.

THE EVOLUTION OF PEACE

As we evolve our thinking, peace stops being merely a theoretical concept and starts to become a genuine, attainable reality. It necessitates acknowledging our common humanity, choosing nonviolence consciously, and creating structures that promote equity, justice, and understanding. The most important step any of us can take as a species is to enable peace, and it starts with each of us.

Do not return harm for harm. Instead, respond with the strength of nonviolence, dignity, and love. Interrupt cycles of hatred and revenge by meeting injustice with a radically different energy—one that seeks transformation, not domination. We must actively work to generate peace rather than waiting for it to come. The path to peace offers a future in which everyone can live with dignity, security, and harmony, making it the most significant evolutionary path we can follow.

We have the courage to change, and by doing so, we have the bravery to establish a peaceful society.

*Give evil nothing to oppose, and it will
disappear by itself.*
~ *Tao Te Ching* STEPHEN MITCHELL, translator

**How can we shift our daily actions and perspectives
to envision sustainable solutions for peace?**

CHAPTER 6

Holistic Health

*"It's better to be the oldest in the gym rather than
the youngest in the nursing home."*

~ UNKNOWN

As a species we have separated ourselves from nature and, within Western Medicine, have constructed the view that health is about "us versus viruses and germs." This model has led us to try to separate every instance of lack of health into a specific problem. Each major organ being treated as a separate system that has to be treated only on its own. The reality is that we are a symphony, not only within the body, but in connection with all of nature. Each piece of nature supporting all others with love that is in congruence with the purpose of the other.

Being disease-free is not the only indicator of health. Living in peace with the environment, one another, and ourselves is a prerequisite for true wellness. The goal of regenerative holistic health is to provide long-term support for resilience and vitality in the body, mind, and spirit. Holistic health aims to promote sustainable well-being from the inside out, restore balance, and support natural healing processes. This approach contrasts with conventional allopathic care, which frequently concentrates on treating symptoms without looking for the actual cause.

To promote resilient lifestyle habits, embrace integrative solutions, and reestablish a connection with traditional healing methods. This chapter delves into novel approaches to regenerative holistic wellness and healthy aging.

This subject greatly interests me. In 1980, my 10-year-old son developed cancer and died less than a month later. He was only diagnosed 4 days before his death. The cancer was doubling in his body every 24 hours. He was an all-star soccer and baseball player, so it was shocking and traumatic. While we will never know the exact cause, in hindsight it seems apparent to me the toxins in the environment, the lack of nutrients in processed foods, and the attitude of Western medicine that the sole treatment is an artificial drug that treats only the symptom not the cause, are the major reasons. Today, 60% of the United States population has a chronic disease, and 40% have 2 or more. Here, I am presenting alternatives I believe can make a difference.

The Secrets of Longevity: *Blue Zones*

People who live to be over 100 years old are known as centenarians, and they are found in extraordinarily large numbers in some areas around the world, referred to as Blue Zones. These areas include places like Loma Linda, California; Sardinia, Italy; and Okinawa, Japan. The secret to understanding how we might achieve healthy aging through holistic living lies in the habits of these communities.

People who live in Blue Zones tend to follow more plant-based diets, exercise frequently, have close-knit social networks, and have a strong sense of purpose or spiritual engagement. The emphasis on complete, unprocessed foods is essential for lowering inflammation and fostering long-term health. Particularly, this applies to foods high in fiber, antioxidants, and healthy fats.

A Blue Zone-inspired lifestyle calls for more than just dietary adjustments. It's about living a slower, more contemplative lifestyle, cultivating meaningful connections, and partaking in consistent, purposeful activities that keep the body and mind engaged well into older age.

Eat Well, Sleep Well, Move Well, Stress Well:
The Foundations of Health

Resilience and energy are gradually built through basic, core habits that constitute true health. These include taking care of oneself by eating a balanced diet, getting enough sleep, exercising frequently, and practicing healthy stress management. Kerry McClure, founder of Practical Wellness, builds her practice around these four principles.

Eat Well: The foundation of regenerative health is nutrition. Fruits, vegetables, whole grains, nuts, and seeds are examples of, plant-based whole foods that supply the body with the nutrition it needs to repair and rejuvenate. Locally grown, organic food further lowers exposure to dangerous chemicals and promotes environmental sustainability.

Prioritize Sleep: During sleep, the body heals, cleanses, and revitalizes itself. Chronic sleep deprivation weakens the immune system, impairs cognitive function, and accelerates aging. Long-term health depends on making sleep a priority, creating a relaxing nighttime ritual, and sleeping in sync with the body's natural circadian rhythms.

Move Well: As we age, preserving our cardiovascular health, muscular strength, and bone density requires regular physical activity. Consistency is more important than intensity when it comes to movement. Exercises that maintain body strength and flexibility, like yoga, swimming, stretching, and walking, all help people live longer.

Manage Stress: Although stress is unavoidable, how we respond to it affects our health. Prolonged stress accelerates the aging process and raises inflammation. Practicing yoga, meditation, and mindfulness on a regular basis can help you maintain balance and improve your mental clarity while managing stress.

"Mindfulness is a pause. It's the space between reaction and response. That's where choice lives."

~ Kerry McClure

The Institute for Functional Medicine

The focus on individualized, systems-based care by the Institute for Functional Medicine (IFM) signifies a revolutionary change in the way that health and wellness are approached. Through customized treatment plans that take lifestyle, environmental, and genetic factors into account, IFM practitioners aim to find and address the underlying causes of chronic disease rather than just treating its symptoms. The idea that the body functions as an interrelated system and that imbalances in one region can affect other areas is fundamental to their methodology. IFM enables practitioners and patients to work together to maximize health outcomes by fusing the most recent scientific findings with holistic healing practices. Their research has shaped a paradigm in healthcare that emphasizes nutrition, prevention, and the body's natural ability to heal.

CLEAR Center of Health

Leading the way in integrative medicine, the CLEAR Center of Health offers individualized treatment by fusing allopathic medicine with complementary natural and regenerative therapies. They provide a comprehensive approach to health that deals with the underlying causes of disease rather than merely its symptoms. Their offerings are centered on fostering long-term wellness via the integration of cutting-edge technology and traditional healing techniques.

Patients are seen as complete individuals at the CLEAR Center, where preventive care is prioritized and patients are given the tools they need to take control of their own health. Among their services are:

Functional Medicine: This approach that use a systems-based methodology to examine the underlying causes of illness. It emphasizes lifestyle aspects such as stress management, exercise, and food. The goal of functional medicine is to correct imbalances that cause illness in order to maximize health.

Herbal Medicine and Nutritional Support: To assist the body's inherent healing processes, The CLEAR Center combines natural therapies, such as herbal medicine, and specialized nutritional regimens.

Detoxification Programs: By helping the body get rid of toxin accumulation due to stress, processed meals, and environmental exposure, their detox programs support general wellness and cellular regeneration.

Mind-Body Therapies: CLEAR Center acknowledges the close relationship between physical and mental well-being. By means of therapies such as yoga, meditation, and counseling, they tackle emotional well-being as an essential constituent of health.

The CLEAR Center of Health is an example of how using energy healing along with functional medicine provides great results. Their integrative approach captures the spirit of holistic care, treating the patient as a whole and laying the groundwork for long-term health. Beth McDougall, M.D., is the founder of CLEAR Center of Health. Her book *Your Pristine Blueprint* is a great read.

JYZEN Labs

JYZEN, located in Mill Valley, California, is a cutting-edge medical and human performance center that integrates advanced bio-optimization technologies with comprehensive integrative medicine. Their mission is to revolutionize healthcare by addressing the root causes of health concerns and enhancing overall well-being. Beth McDougall, MD, is also co-founder of JYZEN Labs.

The center offers a range of services across three key departments:

Brain: Using technologies like 19-channel EEG brain mapping and neuromodulation protocols, JYZEN's NeuroFit® programs aim to heal brain injuries, calm limbic overactivation, and restore autonomic nervous system balance.

Body: The Body Optimization department focuses on structural health, ensuring proper alignment and function of the musculoskeletal system. Services include physical therapy, chiropractic care, and advanced regenerative therapies to enhance physical health and performance.

Biology: JYZEN's integrative medicine department offers deep-level diagnostics, intravenous medicine, hormone balance, peptide therapy, infectious disease treatment, metabolic enhancements, and specialized programs aimed at optimizing biological functions.

By combining these services, JYZEN provides personalized care designed to restore, regenerate, and elevate health, enabling individuals to live vibrant, fulfilling lives.

Ashland Natural Medicine

Ashland Natural Medicine provides a holistic, patient-focused approach to healthcare by combining traditional natural remedies with cutting-edge diagnostic technologies. With a focus on treating the full person—mind, body, and spirit—this integrated clinic in southern Oregon offers customized care with a foundation in naturopathic medicine. Their philosophy focuses on lifestyle-based treatment and preventative care, addressing the underlying causes of illness through advanced testing, homeopathy, botanical medicine, nutritional counseling, and physical medicine

With a focus on enabling patients to actively participate in their own recovery, Ashland Natural Medicine helps patients with a range of ailments, from hormonal abnormalities to chronic exhaustion. Their philosophies are quite similar to those of regenerative health, which holds that healing involves the restoration of life and balance rather than only the absence of sickness. Dr. Chris Chlebowski is the founder and practitioner at Ashland Natural Medicine.

Casey Means, M.D., and *Good Energy*: *Pioneering Holistic Health and Wellness*

Casey Means, MD, a Stanford-trained physician and entrepreneur, is reshaping how we understand and manage health through her innovative approach with *Good Energy*. This initiative is rooted in lifestyle medicine, personalized health insights, and holistic wellness. With a background in otolaryngology and a deep passion for metabolic health,

Dr. Means has dedicated her career to addressing the root causes of chronic disease.

Good Energy promotes the use of data-driven insights to empower individuals in making sustainable lifestyle changes. By integrating cutting-edge technology with evidence-based wellness strategies, the project focuses on enhancing energy, vitality, and long-term well-being. This aligns with Dr. Means' broader mission: to bridge the gap between modern medicine and lifestyle interventions, offering proactive solutions for improved quality of life. To quote her, "Our health is a reflection of what we have done to the Earth."

Through tools like continuous glucose monitoring and educational resources, *Good Energy* helps individuals find more ways to optimize nutrition, movement, and mindfulness, fostering an informed and engaged approach to health. Dr. Means continues to advocate for preventive care, inspiring communities to harness their personal energy to create healthier, more vibrant lives.

Mederi Center: *Integrative Cancer Care*

The Mederi Center is an excellent example of how integrative medicine may be used to treat complicated diseases like cancer. The Mederi Center employs a holistic approach that treats the full person rather than just the ailment by combining traditional and alternative therapies.

With a focus on individualized care that promotes the body's natural ability to heal, the center combines herbal medicine, nutritional therapy, mind-body techniques, and conventional oncology. The regenerative health model that honors both the knowledge of conventional medicine and the latest discoveries in science is reflected in this integrative approach. Donnie Yance is a master herbalist and the founder of Mederi Center.

Riordan Clinic: *Cancer Treatment Adjunct Protocol*
The Intravenous Vitamin C Protocol offered by the Riordan Clinic is another illustration of how regenerative health can enhance conventional medical care. Administering high-concentration intravenous vitamin C is a complementary treatment for cancer that enhances the immune system, lowers inflammation, and supports the body's defense against illness.

High doses of vitamin C have been shown to promote energy, lessen the negative effects of radiation and chemotherapy, and improve quality of life. The larger regenerative health paradigm, which aims to cure illness by promoting the body's natural healing processes, is reflected in this approach.

Mirrors In The Earth
Asia Suler in her book *Mirrors In The Earth* tells the story of how a her journey with health challenges were mitigated through the use of her knowledge of the planet to extract remedial modalities that enabled her healing and also restored her to thriving. This led her to the realization that the renovation of the planet is enabled through our caring and actions that realign with the energy of this world's creation. Her writing is motivational, and it points us to reenabling the communication with our environment.

The Healing Power of Connection: *Hugs and Human Touch*
It is impossible to overstate the value of physical contact. Despite its apparent simplicity, hugging has a significant physiological impact. It lowers blood pressure, strengthens the immune system, and decreases stress hormones. Studies

have shown that embracing someone for at least 20 seconds causes the production of oxytocin, popularly known as the "love hormone," which fortifies emotional ties and fosters sentiments of security and trust. Eight hugs a day are recommended by experts for both physical and mental well-being.

Hugging often isn't only about showing physical affection; it's also about fostering a culture of caring, connecting with loved ones, and developing a sense of community. Hugging someone transforms into a radical gesture of healing and regeneration in a time when loneliness and alienation are on the rise.

At age 67, I had a potentially fatal bicycle accident. I woke up in a ditch with a lady shaking me, asking if I was okay. Upon moving only a little, I knew I was not. had 14 broken bones. I spent 5 days in a trauma unit and 2 weeks in a 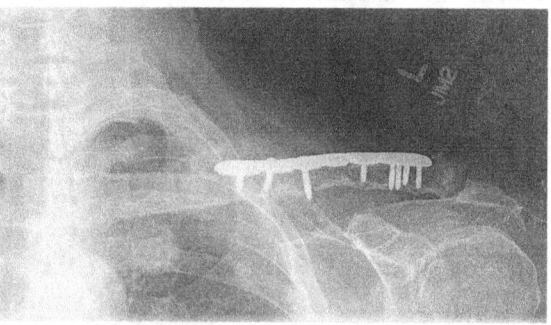 rehab facility. On day 3, I looked at Kerry and said, "This is an opportunity to learn something new about my body." Five weeks after the accident, I wound up having surgery to piece my collarbone back together (they had to rebreak it because it had already started healing). The plate is still in my shoulder. I was fortunate that everything else, while serious, was able to repair itself. I believe that one of the most healing modalities during my recovery was the hugs I received in our community. Hugs provide a special energy. Today I am able to walk 6 to 10 miles every day and have an active lifestyle.

Mindfulness and Meditation: *Cultivating Inner Stillness*
In ancient traditions, mindfulness and meditation were highly valued as means of achieving spiritual development, emotional equilibrium, and mental clarity. These exercises aim to develop a strong bond between the self and the present moment in addition to reducing stress. They have shown results in treating PTSD and trauma.

Anxiety and depression are among the mental health conditions for which mindfulness, the practice of being totally present without passing judgment, has enormous healing potential. Mindfulness helps interrupt the patterns of automatic responses to stress by focusing on the body and breathing, making room for deliberate, intentional responses. According to a regenerative health paradigm, being aware is essential for preserving equilibrium in a hectic environment.

Conversely, meditation delves deeper. It helps us to reestablish our mental and emotional energies by connecting us with a sense of tranquility that surpasses everyday existence. Meditation has been shown to boost immunity, reduce inflammatory responses in the body, and improve sleep—all important aspects of aging healthily. As we develop, meditation turns into a regular practice that helps us live in harmony with our higher consciousness by reestablishing our connection to life's inherent flow.

Yoga: *Balance for Body and Mind*
Yoga is a holistic form of exercise that combines breathing techniques, physical postures, and mental concentration to bring the body and mind into balance. In contrast to traditional exercise, which frequently targets the body's external goals and isolates muscles, yoga promotes conscious movement and a strong sense of self-connection.

Yoga's asanas, or poses, help people become stronger and more flexible and relieve physical tension in ways that support long life. Another gift of yoga is its capacity to quiet the mind and increase awareness of our emotional and physical movements in the environment.

Regular yoga practice increases self-awareness, which is crucial for long-term wellbeing. The flexibility and balance that yoga develops can help us stay mobile as we age, lower our chance of falling, and improve our body's ability to recover itself.

Twelve Principles of Attitudinal Healing

The Twelve Principles of Attitudinal Healing offers a groundbreaking approach to mental and emotional health. These ideas, which were developed by Gerald Jampolsky MD, center on encouraging forgiveness, compassion, and peace as the cornerstones of healing. The guiding principle of this approach is changing the focus from fear to love.

The notion that we have a choice in how we react to life's obstacles lies at the heart of attitudinal rehabilitation. We may lower emotional tension, build resilience, and pave the way for improved physical and mental well-being when we choose to align with love instead of fear. A potent tool in any regenerative health practice, attitudinal healing invites us to view life as a window of opportunities rather than constricted by limitations.

Homeopathy

Homeopathy is a medical system that was developed in Germany more than 200 years ago. It is based on two unconventional principles: the "law of minimum dose," which suggests that the effectiveness of a remedy increases with greater dilution, and "like cures like," which suggests that substances that cause symptoms in healthy people can treat similar symptoms in sick people. There is a new documentary *Introducing Solutions Through Homeopathy* presenting cases where severe illnesses have been put into remission using homeopathy.

Ho'oponopono

Dr. Hew Len, a Hawaiian psychologist, is renowned for using the traditional practice of ho'oponopono, a method of forgiveness and reconciliation, to change the lives of patients in a ward for the criminally insane. This is one of the most powerful examples of healing outside of traditional medicine. Dr. Len went over patient files without actually meeting them, repeating inaudibly, "I'm sorry. Please forgive me. Thank you. I love you." The ward changed over time, releasing shackled inmates, reducing medication use, and ultimately closing the entire section. A radical view of health as a shared energetic field where individual accountability, love, and profound inner purification promote group healing is encouraged by Dr. Len's work. Ho'oponopono invites us to repair the part of ourselves that sees damage in the world, rather than trying to fix other people.

Embracing Regenerative Holistic Health for a Vibrant Future

Regenerative holistic health goes beyond disease prevention. It aims to foster balance, vitality, and a sense of oneness with the natural world. The habits discussed in this chapter provide us with avenues to not only live longer but also live better as we age. These practices—from yoga and mindfulness to the mysteries of the Blue Zones—remind us that maintaining good health requires a lifetime of rejuvenation.

To regenerate our health means honoring the knowledge of historic traditions, embracing technological advancements in a way that benefits the full person, and synchronizing with the cycles of nature. We are blessed to live in a time where we look at the whole organism, not only at isolated symptoms, to find the source on an illness. We need to take personal responsibility for our well-being and dare to adapt, so that we can set off a chain reaction that helps the Earth and all of its inhabitants to regenerate. May we do so with love.

How can we shift our daily actions and perspectives to consider sustainable solutions for health?

CHAPTER 7

Love and Compassion

*"Love and compassion are necessities, not luxuries.
Without them, humanity cannot survive."*

~ DALAI LAMA in *The Art of Happiness*

Love and compassion are the foundation of living in harmony with the world and one another; they are more than just feelings. Love and compassion are potent catalysts for healing, connection, and transformation in a time when division frequently rules the world story. There are numerous social, environmental, and spiritual initiatives based on love and compassion that aim to build a more equitable and sustainable world. This chapter will examine numerous international initiatives that are devoted to compassion and love. Providing an overview of how these forces influence societies, promote understanding, and eventually move us closer to a future where conflict resolution allows everyone to live in the possibility of peace and harmony.

There is a source that enables all that is. It does so using love and compassion, with the intention of enabling the highest potential. Each person gets to then decide if they individually are going to support that prospective.

On the day my son passed away, we returned to our home and informed my parents, who were in town to help out. Later, we realized we did not have any food for dinner. Still in somewhat of a daze from the events of the day, I went to the store. I was standing in line to check out, and there were probably seven or eight people in front of me. I realized that none of them knew what I had experienced that day, and I did not know what they had experienced that day either. This realization was a catalyst that motivated me to find a new way of engaging with other people. People are going about their day and, in general, are preoccupied with their current concerns. This experience made it clear to me that being kind in my interactions was a compassionate and loving thing to do. It is a transition that still takes time and effort, but I have found that being polite, kind, and curious is a great way to move in the world. It enables new friends and the opportunity to learn many new things. As Valarie Kaur often says, "You are a part of me I do not yet know."

HeartMath: *The Science of Heart-Centered Living*

The HeartMath Institute is a leader in the study of the heart's impact on our physical and mental health. HeartMath emphasizes heart-centered living by demonstrating how techniques like heart coherence can foster love and compassion. The program is based on the theory that the heart produces a strong electromagnetic field.

Heart coherence is achieving physiological balance and emotional stability by synchronizing the heart's rhythms with feelings of gratitude, love, and compassion. Globally, people use HeartMath's tools and practices to lower stress, improve health, and strengthen interpersonal connections. Their findings show that people can change their own emotional states and have a good impact on those around them by concentrating on love and compassion.

HeartMath has demonstrated that heart-centered emotions like love and compassion can have a positive ripple effect on collective consciousness in addition to improving personal well-being. Using technology to measure the electromagnetic field of the heart and reporting that to the person permits them to lower their stress levels.

Revolutionary Love: *A Global Movement for Compassion*

At the risk of being repetitive, I am including the work of Valarie Kaur in this area again. Her work is so inclusive in its scope that I feel it needs to be presented under both of the subject areas.

Valarie Kaur, a writer and activist, founded the Revolutionary Love Project with the belief that love can be a powerful force for social justice. According to Kaur, love is a bold act of resistance as well as an emotion that has the power to end both individual and societal suffering. The Revolutionary Love Project envisions a society in which people make a commitment to love themselves, their opponents, and each other.

Through her work, Kaur encourages people to see love as a proactive tool for mending society's profound rifts. She teaches that we may contribute to the renovation of the violent and hateful systems that cause suffering by making the decision to love and care for everyone, even our opponents. The Revolutionary Love Project provides instruction, materials, and seminars to support people in their practice of radical love as a strategy for transforming society.

The Compassion Project: *Teaching Empathy to the Next Generation*

The Compassion Project is one of the most effective initiatives to promote compassion because it teaches kindness and empathy to young children. This effort, based on the idea that empathy can be developed via education, collaborates with educational institutions worldwide to include empathy training in the curriculum.

The Compassion Project uses tales, exercises, and lessons to help kids learn empathy, become more emotionally intelligent, and act with compassion. The project aims to raise a future generation that values kindness over cruelty and connection over conflict by sowing the seeds of empathy at a young age.

The Compassion Project is changing how children connect with each other and creating a culture of caring that goes well beyond the classroom thanks to its widespread adoption in schools. This movement shows that compassion is a talent that can be learned, developed, and practiced in addition to being an innate quality.

On Being: *Compassion as a Way of Life*

Krista Tippett hosts the podcast and public radio program On Being, which delves into the nexus of philosophy, spirituality, and humanity. On Being explores the deeper concerns of existence through introspective talks with academics, poets, scientists, and religious leaders. Compassion is frequently at the center of these talks.

Tippett's work offers viewpoints from a diverse range of voices and traditions, encouraging listeners to consider what it means to live a compassionate life. Every discussion shines light on how compassion can be developed as a method of being in the world as well as an emotion. The podcast On Being serves as a helpful reminder that practicing compassion is something that can be done through introspection, discussion, and action.

On Being has inspired millions of listeners to consider how they can incorporate more love and compassion into their lives, communities, and interactions with others.

Radical Compassion: *A Path to Healing and Reconciliation*

Author and psychotherapist Tara Brach, PhD, popularized the idea of *Radical Compassion*, which advocates for a more profound comprehension of compassion as a means of promoting both individual and group healing. Beyond mere empathy, radical compassion asks us to love ourselves and others, even during painful and contentious times, and to accept even the most challenging feelings.

The RAIN technique, which stands for Recognize, Allow, Investigate, and Nurture, is the main topic of Dr. Brach's lessons. This approach, encourages people to identify their emotions, accept them as they are, explore within their own life, and then care for themselves with compassion. People can use this approach to heal from severe emotional scars and increase compassion in their interpersonal connections.

Radical compassion is not just about feeling for others—it's about transforming how we relate to ourselves and the world. Dr. Brach's work emphasizes that in practicing compassion for ourselves, we become more capable of extending it to others. Her teachings have helped many people move through trauma, offering a path to healing that centers on love and acceptance.

THE POWER OF LOVE AND COMPASSION TO HEAL THE WORLD

Love and compassion are not merely abstract concepts; they are powerful forces capable of transforming individuals and in turn, societies. The movements and projects discussed in this chapter demonstrate how these qualities can be cultivated, practiced, and applied to heal divisions, promote social justice, and create a more connected and compassionate world.

As we dare to evolve, love and compassion become central to our journey. These forces invite us to live in alignment with our highest values, to see ourselves in others, and to act in ways that promote healing rather than harm. The global projects dedicated to love and compassion offer a blueprint for how we can live more intentionally, creating a ripple effect that extends far beyond ourselves.

By choosing love and compassion as guiding principles in our lives, we take responsibility not only for our own well-being but for the well-being of all people. In doing so, we contribute to the regeneration of humanity, helping to build a world where peace, understanding, and kindness flourish.

"Love begins with wonder."
~ VALARIE KAUR

In every interaction, every choice, we have the opportunity to embody these values and be the change we wish to see. The future of our planet depends on it.

How can we shift our daily actions and perspectives to foster love and compassion around us?

CHAPTER 8

We Are One

"All differences in this world are of degree, and not of kind, because oneness is the secret of everything."

~ SWAMI VIVEKANANDA

The evolution of a human to be a divine entity with the ability to taste, smell, see, hear, and be in congruency with our planet is a miracle. We are here to wake up every day to imagine how we can enlighten ourselves and, by being that, enable a higher purpose for all. How and why has the planet evolved humans to have these abilities? It is now our responsibility to empower these interactive faculties in alignment with the purpose that evolution developed in bringing us to this point. In my daily activities, how do I allow the connection with all that is in each moment? May we experience the wonder and embrace it. It is within our potential to protect and embrace all species on the planet.

The idea that we are one shines as a ray of hope in a world where division has shattered relationships. It is a reminder of our innate connectedness to all living things. The same threads that hold the Earth together bind us together, not the other way around. This concept is fundamental to our orientation to life, relationships, and our surroundings; it goes beyond a purely spiritual perspective. To build a future in which harmony and sustainability are achievable, it is essential that we acknowledge our unity with the Earth and with one another.

We have to acknowledge this unity before we can bring equilibrium with all of nature back. Our decisions shift as we recognize that we are a part of the ecosystems, communities, and lives that surround us. We now act out of love and responsibility for all life, not out of selfishness or the desire for immediate gain. The message's core is this: we are one

For me, this concept came to me naturally in the early years of my life. Then it became something I had trouble accepting, as everything seemed separate. As I had experiences where I felt my higher potential, whether physical, mental, emotional, or otherwise, I related more and more to being at one with everything. As I walk in the park, I feel the ion energy of the creek with its swift current. The beauty of the light on the path, the trees and the undergrowth as it changes with clouds passing overhead and then the sun emerging to enhance each shadow in a magical way. I experience trees sharing their energy, and I feel love back toward them for all they provide to support humans as well as everything else. These experiences lead me to be open and try to work through the divisions that are so polarizing in many areas of life today. This is when I know that I am at unity with everything that is! The true blessing of knowing from the vibration of my being; we are one.It gives me great hope for a future that supports all life.

Additionally, experiencing high-energy environments such as Sedona, AZ, and Mount Shasta in California, makes it clear that our intellect needs to step aside and allow our being to meld with all that is.

EVERYTHING IS ENERGY

The realization that everything is made of energy forms the basis of our awareness of our interconnectivity. There is a constant interchange and transformation of energy, starting from the Sun, which powers plant development, and continuing down the food chain with nutrients. People are a part of this energy flow as well. There is energy in our ideas, feelings, and deeds that is released into the universe.

We become more deliberate with our energy when we understand that every action we take, no matter how tiny, has an impact on the larger picture. The long-term effects of wastefulness, greed, and exploitation start to become less appealing. Realizing that we are energetic beings within a larger energy system helps us act in a way that is more compassionate and regenerative.

There are a number of authors that have explored the concept of unity. Their insights into our connection with the universe have supported my evolution in thinking regarding we are one.

Mind to Matter: The Power of Thought

In *Mind to Matter* by Dawson Church reinforced what I had already begun to suspect, how our thoughts shape the reality around us. Our minds are directly responsible for generating the world we live in, not something distinct from it. This concept goes beyond philosophical theory. It's a useful insight into how directed intention and uplifting energy can produce observable results.

The mental transition from division and fear to love and oneness starts here. Knowing that our thoughts matter gives us the ability to nurture ideas that uphold our highest ideals—thoughts that reaffirm our unity with the planet and one another. By doing so, we help to create a world that is representative of those ideals.

The Reality We Create

The reality we create as a collective is largely reflected in the world in which we live. The idea that our decisions, ideas, and perceptions create the environment we live in is highlighted in *The Reality We Create* by Warren L. Cargal, L.Ac.. We will build systems that mirror our perception of ourselves as disparate from the natural world and from one another—systems based on rivalry, devastation, and imbalance.

However, our reality changes if we start to perceive the world as interrelated. We begin constructing systems that demonstrate cooperation, renewal, and equilibrium. We must actively construct a new world by acting as though we are already a part of it.

Effortless Mind: **A Path to Peace**

Understanding that our minds shape reality, as discussed in *Mind to Matter*, naturally leads to the question: How do we quiet the mind to align with this reality? *Effortless Mind* by Ajayan Borys examines how to quiet the mind to access life's more profound flow. The constant barrage of tasks, tension, and diversions from our actual selves and the outside world are often the sounds of everyday existence. However, we may better hear and harmonize with nature's subtle knowledge when we practice an easy mind.

A mind at ease is not inert; rather, it is responsive and open. It enables us to respond to life with congruency in mind, instead of just reacting to it. To truly live up to the idea that we are all one, this change is essential. We can better understand our connection to the whole and live in accordance with it when we can still our inner chatter.

On a silent retreat in the Himalayas Ajayan was approached by a swami in the forest who recognized he was doing a silent meditation. The swami remarked that life without meditation was like a string of zeros. By adding meditation to your life, it is putting a 1 at the beginning of all those zeros.

The Way of Vastu: Harmony with Space

How do we enable our immediate environment to support the quiet mind. Vastu, an ancient tradition, shows us how to coexist peacefully with the places around us. Vastu is about designing spaces that promote our well-being and strengthen our ties to the planet, not merely about how buildings are constructed. We may build environments that support and foster life by arranging our living spaces to be in harmony with the natural flow of energy. Robin and Michael Mastro bring practical suggestions for use on this ageless wisdom in *The Way of Vastu.*

We honor the Earth and ourselves when we create our surroundings thoughtfully. Living places become sacred, serving as a constant reminder of our interconnected-ness with all life. This exercise serves to reaffirm that our commitment to harmony and balance is reflected in every decision we make, including the design of our houses.

Altars of Power and Grace: Sacred Spaces of Connection

From harmony to sacred, the book *Altars of Power and Grace* by Robin and Michael Mastro challenges us to design sacred places where we can establish connections with the divine, the Earth, and ourselves. These altars provide a space for us to stop, think, and reconnect with the values of compassion and harmony while also acting as symbols of our interconnectedness.

By building altars, real or imagined, we firmly establish our ties to the idea that everything is interconnected. These hallowed spaces turn into wellsprings of courage and understanding, reminding us that we are never really alone. Every decision we make and every idea we have has an impact on the entire web of existence.

Celebrate Your Divinity: Embracing the Sacred Within

Bringing it again to this sacred being we are, we must acknowledge our own divinity before we can fully accept the idea that we are all one. *Celebrate Your Divinity* by Orest Bedrij shows us that we may respect others' sanctity more fully if we first recognize our own sacredness. We perceive the environment as divine when we perceive ourselves as divine.

This insight creates a significant change in how we relate to each other and the environment. It takes us from a mindset of shortage and fear to one of abundance and love. When we see the sacred in everything, we inevitably start acting as stewards of the Earth, guardians of life, and peace activists.

The Greatest Achievement: Unity as a Way of Being

Unity adds to the divinity. Unity enables living in harmony with the Earth Orest Bedrij points out, and is our greatest accomplishment as a species, not conquering or dominating the environment. The understanding that we are all connected to life is the greatest achievement, not the advancement of technology or material wealth. This realization changes the way we live, interact with one another, and treat the environment.

When we embrace our oneness, environmental issues no longer feel distant – they become personal. Because we are a part of the whole, we perceive it as happening to us. Creating a world in which this understanding informs every choice we make will be our greatest accomplishment.

See No Stranger: The Practice of Radical Compassion

We discover the discipline of profound compassion in *See No Stranger* by Valarie Kaur. Seeing no stranger entails acknowledging each individual we encounter as a fellow human being and seeing them as a part of ourselves. This is not just for people; it also applies to the Earth, animals, and all living things.

The idea that we are all one is embodied in radical compassion. It exhorts us to be kind, stand up for those in need, and to bring harmony back wherever it has been disturbed. Radical compassion is a practice that makes us actively involved in the world's healing.

Sage Warrior: The Courage to Protect

Someone who exemplifies strength and wisdom in equal measure is known as a sage warrior. It takes courage to defend the Earth and all of its inhabitants as well as insight to recognize the intertwined nature of all life. Valarie Kaur reminds us that we assume the role of Earth's guardianship as sage warriors, not out of fear but out of love.

The bravery to speak up for what is right, even when it is unpleasant, is a necessary skill for this calling. It demands action based on mutual respect and understanding. A sage warrior understands that the forces of division and devastation are the ones facing them, not other people. Our most powerful tools in this battle are compassion, love, and solidarity.

Institute of Noetic Sciences: *Bridging Science and Spirituality*

The Institute of Noetic Sciences investigates the relationship between spirituality and science, demonstrating how closely related they are rather than distinct. The Institute teaches, explores, and conducts research to help us comprehend how consciousness shapes our reality.

The institute offers insights into how we might progress as a society and as individuals by researching the nature of consciousness. Their research serves as a reminder that spirituality and science both lead to the same conclusion: we are all one. The secret to building a future in which all life can flourish is realizing this fact.

THE COURAGE TO RECOGNIZE OUR ONENESS

Realizing that we are all one requires a change in more than just how we think—it requires a change in our being. Embracing the truth of our connectivity and letting go of the illusion of separateness takes courage. We start to live in a way that respects all life when we realize that every decision we make has an impact on the whole.

The books and ideas shared in this chapter urge us to live out the reality of our unity. They encourage us to behave responsibly, lovingly, and with compassion in the world. We enter the realization that we are a part of the Earth, of one another, and of the divine when we dare to evolve. Everybody is a member of the same divine web of existence.

By embracing this reality, we build a future in which everyone can live in harmony and balance and where every decision advances the welfare of all. By realizing that we are all one, we start the process of healing the planet.

As we embrace the truth that we are all one, we must ask ourselves:

How can we shift our daily actions and mindset to nurture harmony with the world around us?

"Imagine, Create, Play, Share, Reflect, Imagine, Create"

~ MITCHEL RESNICK
Lifelong Kindergarten - Encouraging Creativity to Maintain Genius

CHAPTER 9

Education

The human ability to learn, create, and experience the joy of knowledge in context is a blessing. Each of us is challenged to change when faced with new information, and we experience a cognitive shift. Each time I am aware of this experience in my own life, I become in awe of how the universe enables the knowing of itself.

One of the most effective instruments at our disposal for influencing the future is education. However, the world's existing educational systems—which were first created for the industrial era—often ignore our natural experiential learning abilities and inhibit the very traits that are necessary to overcome the difficult problems of our day, such as creativity, curiosity, and critical thinking. The one-size-fits-all approach, standardized testing, and conformity that characterize modern educational institutions can stifle students' innate brilliance and inventiveness.

It is time to discuss the need to reimagine the future of education so we can preserve the inherent genius that each and every human being possesses, as well as to encourage creativity and lifelong learning.

ENCOURAGE AND ENABLE STUDENT CREATIVITY AND EXPERIENTIAL LEARNING

The fact that standardized responses are frequently valued over original problem-solving techniques is one of the biggest obstacles facing modern education. In our rapidly evolving world, where issues like social inequity, techno-logical disruption, and climate change demand creative and critical thinking, it is crucial to have both critical and creative thinking skills. We need an educational system that not only imparts knowledge but also encourages creativity through experiential learning at every level if we are to preserve children's innate abilities.

In this sense, creativity isn't limited to the arts, though the arts are certainly vital; it also includes the capacity to question conventional wisdom, view issues from fresh angles, and come up with novel solutions. Providing children with opportunities to experiment, ask questions, and fail without fear of punishment is essential to fostering creativity and outside-the-box solutions in the classroom.

NASA Study: *Education Dumbs Down Geniuses*

In a fascinating NASA study, Drs. George Land and Beth Jarman evaluated children's capacity for creative thought across time. The results were astounding: 98% of children between the ages of 4 and 5 years showed genius-level inventiveness, but only 2% of them carried that degree of creativity into adulthood. The evidence unequivocally demonstrates how the existing educational model undervalues youngsters' innate capacity for creativity and critical thinking.

Significant ramifications stem from this research. We must alter the educational system if it is purposefully hindering children's creativity and critical thinking skills. In classrooms, creativity with experimentation should be encouraged and expanded rather than suppressed. Rethinking curriculum design, enabling more project-based learning, promoting critical inquiry, and creating opportunities for interdisciplinary learning—where students can investigate links between seemingly unrelated fields—are some of the steps involved in achieving this.

Overcoming the current public-school biases is difficult, but there are potential innovations. One example is the Worldview Explorations curriculum which a friend of mine volunteered time to help develop at the Institute of Noetic Sciences (IONS) in Petaluma, CA. It is geared towards middle and high school students.

Creative Education Foundation: *Pioneering Creative Thinking*

The value of creativity in education has long been acknowledged by the Creative Education Foundation (CEF). The CEF was founded to encourage creative problem-solving and provides tools, workshops, and initiatives to support teachers and students in realizing their creative potential. The group promotes active problem-solving in the classroom, where students participate in creative processes that result in invention, as an alternative to rote memorization.

This method not only gives children more self-assurance in their creative abilities but also helps them acquire the abilities needed to solve challenges in the real world. With an uncertain future when many of the occupations of tomorrow do not yet exist, encouraging innovation in pupils is essential.

Creativity, Culture and Education: *Building Creative Learning Communities*

An organization called Creativity Culture and Education (CCE) incorporates the arts and culture into the educational process to highlight the value of creativity in education. They work with schools to establish learning settings where creativity and questioning is not an afterthought but rather an integral element of the educational process. The organization fosters children's creative thinking and problem-solving skills by integrating the arts into regular education.

The CCE approach also emphasizes the value of a creative learning community, in which students work together, exchange ideas, and complement one another's skills. In contrast to the competitive, high-stakes testing atmosphere that many students encounter today, this cooperative inquisitive education paradigm offers a more nurturing and stimulating environment for developing creativity.

Home Schooling: *A Personalized Approach*

For students whose creative needs might not be satisfied in typical educational environments, homeschooling provides a potent option. By tailoring educational experiences to a child's interests and passions, families can facilitate deeper investigation and self-directed learning through homeschooling. Students who receive this individualized instruction typically exhibit higher levels of questioning, engagement, creativity, and independence.

The adaptability of home education also makes experiential learning possible, allowing kids to learn through actual events rather than merely reading textbooks. A student who is interested in environmental science, for instance, could spend a day conducting experiments, visiting with experts in the subject, or observing ecosystems. By fostering curiosity and creativity, this hands-on approach helps preserve each students innate brilliance. One of the challenges with this approach is that it requires a parent to be at home doing the teaching. This can be challenging for two working adults and for single parent families.

A local parent using homeschooling has been frustrated with the time requirements and commitment. Her and other parents who are challenged by the responsibility to home-school formed a separate school. They hired a teacher to provide the delivery of the subject curriculum requirements. They were trying to grow the school but could not do it in a time frame that would work for the instructor, so they had to shut it down. There is another Waldorf opportunity (see below) for her daughter next year with some personal home-schooling supporting that, so it is still a challenge. Her son has been back in public school, but it is not serving his needs, so there is ongoing discussion on what form the next steps in his education should take. It is bothersome to watch parents experience these trials. In today's world, it is difficult for most parents to have the freedom to work with others and enable alternatives that are serving their children.

Trails Outdoor School

Ashland, Oregon's Trails Outdoor School provides an educational approach that re-establishes pupils' connection to nature. The school K-8 incorporates outdoor exploration, environmental stewardship, and community building into a standards-based curriculum. It is founded on the idea that learning occurs best when it is experienced firsthand. Students at Trails develop their academic knowledge in the context of the ecosystems they live in, whether they are working on projects about fire ecology and water cycles, caring for the school garden, or journaling under oak canopies. The school fosters not only intellectual growth but also emotional intelligence and responsibility through its guiding principles, which include respect for oneself, others, and the environment. We are reminded that education can be a rooted, regenerative act by this integrative, place-based approach, which fosters deep curiosity and agency.

Waldorf Education

Rudolf Steiner established Waldorf education in the early 1900s. It provides a comprehensive approach that supports each child's head, heart, and hands. Based on the cycles of nature and human growth, Waldorf schools design learning spaces that are incredibly creative, inventive, and vibrant. Storytelling, music, dance, and hands-on crafts are used to combine subjects, assisting pupils in internalizing meaning as well as absorbing information. Early childhood education purposefully delays technology to allow for awe and embodied learning. In order to regenerate our world, the Waldorf method fosters moral responsibility, emotional depth, and free thought.

Waldorf encourages a return to wholeness, where learning develops like a garden: season by season, founded on relationships, in an era when education frequently speeds toward abstract material and digital efficiency.

Generational Conversations: *Learning Through Dialogue*

The knowledge and experience of elder generations is frequently disregarded in the fast-paced modern world. However, talks between younger and older generations, known as generational conversations, can offer priceless educational opportunities that stimulate originality and creativity. Through these discussions students can acquire historical perspectives, learn how problems were solved in various times, and get inspiration from the experiences of people who have lived through important events through these discussions.

In addition to removing barriers across age groups, generational exchanges can foster greater interconnectedness and collaboration in the classroom. Conversations with older generations can help younger generations understand challenges in new ways and imagine solutions they might not have thought of otherwise. Older generations have a lot to give, from life philosophies to practical knowledge.

Likewise older generations may be reenergized by younger generations, and thus embark upon new innovative endeavors. These exchanges could inspire solutions to some of the many issues that have slipped by as we age. Many of which are frustrating problems for the younger generations. Let us all be open to hearing something new, considering possibilities and acting together accordingly.

Khan Academy: *Free World Class Education*

The emergence of Khan Academy, an online platform that facilitates access to high-quality education, has been one of the most revolutionary breakthroughs in education. Khan Academy offers free courses in anything from computer programming to mathematics. Students can study at their own pace, exploring subjects that pique their interest and going over challenging material again when necessary.

With this individualized learning paradigm, students may take charge of their education and develop their creative skills. Without the inflexible schedules of a typical classroom students are allowed to experiment with new subjects, delve deeper into their passions, and cultivate a lifetime love of learning.

Udemy Online Courses: *Lifelong Learning for Creativity*

Another strong platform is Udemy, which offers access to a variety of courses in subjects like art, photography, data analysis and coding. Udemy promotes a lifelong learning model by providing accessible, on-demand learning opportunities.

This encourages people to continue learning new skills and pursuing their creative interests well into adulthood.

The flexibility for students to select courses that align with their career and personal objectives is what makes Udemy unique. Udemy enables students to view education as a creative activity, promoting experimentation and exploration, regardless of whether they want to build new skills for a career transition or are just interested in exploring a hobby.

Schumacher College: *An Ecological and Creative Approach to Learning*

Schumacher College is renowned for its ecologically conscious, comprehensive teaching methodology. This multidisciplinary university combines philosophy, science, and the arts to provide students with a distinctive learning environment that encourages environmental stewardship and creative thinking. The college's curriculum encourages students to approach global concerns from a systems viewpoint, recognizing the interdependence of problems like socioeconomic inequity, biodiversity loss, and climate change.

Schumacher College prepares students to be leaders in their professions by encouraging creative thinking and teamwork. These skills enable students to tackle challenging issues and come up with novel solutions. The college's emphasis on sustainability also aligns with the growing demand for education to emphasize creative action for a better future.

The Foundation for Critical Thinking: *Cultivating Creative Problem Solvers*

Teaching pupils how to think, rather than what to believe, is crucial, according to the Foundation for Critical Thinking. Critical and creative thinking skills are more vital than ever, since we live in a society where disinformation is pervasive and issues are becoming more complicated.

Critical thinking develops the creative reasoning that is necessary to address today's global concerns. Training students to challenge presumptions, evaluate arguments, and generate original ideas builds these skills. It gives children the ability to think beyond the box and create original solutions that are supported by facts and reasoning.

THE WAY FORWARD: EDUCATION FOR A CREATIVE FUTURE

It's evident that encouraging creativity is essential as we reevaluate education. The problems of the 21st century demand creative thinking, problem-solving skills, and the capacity to adjust to a rapidly changing world. In addition to preparing students for the future, an education system that values innovation, preserves student brilliance, and promotes lifelong learning will also give them the ability to influence it.

We can produce a generation of children and young adults who are not only learners but also creators, innovators, and leaders by incorporating creativity into the curriculum, providing flexible learning pathways, and promoting interdisciplinary methods. By making these techniques available to all ages we embrace the potential for a world where solutions evolve across generations. We have the audacity to advance education and, in doing so, to unleash the creative potential of humankind.

It is imperative we keep education up-to-date by giving pupils the tools they need to learn not only what we know now but also how to solve problems in the future.

How can we shift our daily actions and perspectives to reflect on sustainable solutions for education?

*"The Universe doesn't speak English.
It speaks frequency."*

~ NASSIM HARAMEIN

CHAPTER 10

Resonance

I am somewhat aware of my own resonance with the rest of the universe. It is there, but I am not as tuned in as I would like to be. When I am lucky enough to allow myself to be, I experience the relationship with all that is. I am very hopeful for a future that can enable peace, health, and prosperity for all. I know intuitively that this is possible. How can I go about opening my mind and becoming aware of and unlearning those things that do not support our highest purpose? Then encouraging myself to relearn with the mindset of finding that which is in resonance with all? Throughout all that follows here on resonance, there is an implied spiritual energy that is love. Love for working together toward the highest potential in whatever way may support all of us as one.

UNDERSTANDING RESONANCE

Timing and frequency can interact to produce an energy ripple that intensifies effects and promotes harmonious system operation. Resonance serves as a link between the physical and ecological domains, bringing diverse materials together to form a cohesive rhythm.

Resonance in Physics

In physics, resonance is the phenomenon when a vibrating system or an external force makes another system to oscillate at a particular frequency with increased amplitude. When a child is on a swing, their velocity increases with each push, resulting in ever-higher arcs. This is not just a playground principle. By using it in the design of buildings such as skyscrapers and bridges, engineers can prevent damaging vibrations caused by natural resonances.

However, resonance isn't just used in these kinds of general situations. Resonance can be used to maximize the energy contained in vibrating systems, such as sound waves, electromagnetic waves, or even atomic particles. Innovations in fields like wireless energy transfer and accurate measuring instruments like atomic clocks have resulted from this potential. It's a natural occurrence that, when understood, enables effective energy amplification or capture.

Ecological Resonance

Resonance manifests as cycles and rhythms in the natural world. The innate resonance of nature may be seen in everything from the humming of bees to the synchronized pulses of fireflies to the cycles of ocean currents and tides. Every living thing, be it a tree swaying in the breeze or a bird migrating, adjusts its life cycle to match the rhythm of the planet. This harmony serves as a survival mechanism in addition to being lyrical.

Ecological resonance principles are also being used to enhance our understanding of ecosystem functioning. For example, knowing the resonance frequencies of water systems' currents can aid in the construction of more effective tidal energy collection equipment. Ecosystem resonance can provide feedback loops that can destabilize or stabilize an environment, offering guidance on how to bring degraded habitats back into balance.

HARNESSING RESONANCE: INNOVATIONS AND COMPANIES LEADING THE WAY

Resonance is a promising proposition for future practical uses. Businesses are using resonance principles more and more to drive innovation in areas including ecological restoration, human health, and energy harvesting.

Energy Harvesting The International Space Foundation previously the Resonance Science Foundation have investigated the deep relationship between resonance and the structure of the cosmos through Nassim Haramein and his team's work. Their theories explore the notion that resonance is essential in forming the structure of space-time itself and that the entire universe functions through interconnected fields of energy. According to the team's research, the world vibrates at the tiniest scales with a single, unified field connecting everything in a synchronized dance of frequencies, from subatomic particles to galaxies. They contend that a comprehension of these resonant patterns may lead to fresh perspectives on the creation of energy, gravitation, and matter itself.

As for applying these ideas, they envision technologies that are in tune with the natural rhythms of the universe, potentially leading to breakthroughs in space exploration and sustainable energy. By tapping into the universe's innate resonance, humanity may be able to access new energy sources and gain a better understanding of our place in it.

Wireless Energy Transfer Firms are developing wireless energy transfer devices by leveraging resonance in electromagnetic fields. One such inventor is WiTricity, which has developed technology that allows energy to be transported wirelessly across small distances. This resonant induction-based technology has the potential to revolutionize the way we power everything from electric cars to household appliances.

Health and Well-Being

The idea of resonance is also applied to human health, where it is employed in treatments aimed at restoring homeostasis in the body. The CLEAR Center of Health has been investigating the potential benefits of particular frequencies for general well-being and stress reduction. Resonant frequencies are used in sound therapy, which is becoming more and more popular as a method for encouraging physical and mental relaxation by bringing the body's inherent rhythms into harmony.

JYZEN Labs employs a similar approach, fusing traditional knowledge with cutting-edge technology, by evaluating and readjusting body frequencies through bio-resonance methods to promote optimal health. The concept is straightforward but profound: there is more possibility for healing and vitality when our cells and systems are vibrating at their ideal frequencies.

Businesses such as the Resonant Technologies Group are investigating methods to harvest ambient vibrations and transform them into energy that may be used in many ways. For example, health and ecological settings, to mention only two. Applications for this approach range from the development of frequency products that support health issues to using electromagnetic information that enables better crop yields and water usage.

THE FUTURE OF RESONANCE

The potential applications of resonance in several fields are increasing along with our understanding of it. Resonance provides a route to a more peaceful and sustainable society, whether it is used to create non-invasive health treatments, harness the soft sway of ocean waves to create energy, or restore ecosystems to balance. It holds the key to opening up new vistas for creativity and well-being for those who have the courage to delve into it.

We learn from resonance that harmony is a real force rather than merely an idea. One wave, one vibration, one heartbeat at a time, we discover methods to increase life's vibrancy as we become attuned to its rhythms.

How can we shift our daily actions and perspectives to reflect on ways to support resonance?

"Good design is sustainable design."

~ IMRAN AMED

CHAPTER 11

Regenerative Buildings

The structures in which we work and live have a significant effect on the environment and our health. In light of resource depletion and climate change, the construction sector needs to move past its historical methods of resource exploitation, and ecosystem pollution. Sustainable buildings, on the other hand, go beyond minimizing harm to actively regenerate and restore the environment. By using eco-friendly technologies, energy-efficient designs, and sustainable materials, these structures are intended to complement nature rather than compete with it. They stand for a new paradigm in architecture, one that sees structures as living organisms that improve the well-being of their occupants as well as the Earth. We are daring ourselves to evolve.

After my son's death, I had a difficult time getting my concentration back. My employer was generous and gave me some time off as a medical leave. During that time, I had the opportunity to purchase a solar water heater system with panels. It gave me the chance to use my energy on something that greatly interested me. It was hard physical labor, and I also used some of the skills my father had taught me, such as soldering pipes for plumbing. It was a blessing and, at the same time, challenging. Working on that system allowed me to engage both my intellect and physical skills, which helped me to recover so I could return to work. Plus, our home gas bill was reduced because most of the hot water was produced with solar energy.

U.S. Green Building Council (USGBC)

Through its LEED (Leadership in Energy and Environmental Design) certification program, the US Green Building Council (USGBC) has been leading the way in promoting sustainable building methods. Global green construction standards are established by LEED, which addresses everything from indoor air quality and sustainable material use to energy efficiency and water conservation.

In addition to being energy-efficient, a building that has earned a LEED certification has been designed with its occupants' well-being in mind. It uses renewable energy sources, lessens water waste, and gives priority to natural light. In order to reduce the ecological impact of construction, many of the materials used in these structures are recycled, locally sourced, or sustainably obtained. Builders may help restore natural resources and guarantee a healthier environment for coming generations by implementing LEED requirements.

World Green Building Council

The World Green Building Council (WorldGBC) is spearheading global efforts to significantly cut carbon emissions from the building industry to accelerate the shift toward sustainable development. Their analysis indicates that buildings are a major target in the fight against climate change, accounting for close to 40% of worldwide carbon emissions.

The WorldGBC's Net Zero Carbon Buildings Commitment has challenged governments, architects, and construction companies to completely eradicate operational carbon emissions by the year 2050. This entails the use of sustainable materials, renewable energy sources, and energy-efficient designs. Net-zero buildings generate as much energy as they consume, frequently with the help of on-site renewable energy sources including geothermal, wind, and solar power.

Regenerative structures planned with this dedication in mind accomplish more than just using less energy. When they incorporate green roofs, vegetated walls, and urban trees, they serve as carbon sinks that absorb carbon dioxide and replenish biodiversity. They can also, in many cases, provide high-nutrition foods when designed appropriately.

EPA Green Buildings: *The Role of Government in Sustainable Construction*

Government policies and directives significantly influence how the building sector approaches sustainability. Green building rules from the U. S. Environmental Protection Agency (EPA) encourage using sustainable materials, minimizing waste, and building for energy efficiency.

Eco-friendly materials included in EPA-certified buildings include bamboo, repurposed wood, recycled steel, and paints and coatings with minimal volatile organic compounds (VOCs). These materials boost occupant health by lowering the building's detrimental footprint and enhancing indoor air quality. Furthermore, water-saving technology that drastically lowers water consumption—like rainwater harvesting systems and greywater recycling—are encouraged by EPA rules.

These official directives emphasize the necessity of regenerative building design techniques, guaranteeing that all building projects align with environmental sustainability objectives.

Nano Tech Materials: *Revolutionizing Green Building Materials*

The regenerative construction movement depends on innovations in building materials, and one such development is Nano Tech Materials. Made of nanoparticles, nanotech coatings are intended to improve a building's resilience, energy economy, and environmental impact. By protecting against fire, reflecting heat, lowering the demand for air conditioning, and shielding buildings from UV rays, these coatings can increase a building's lifespan and lower maintenance expenses.

With the ability to create more resilient, energy-efficient, and ecologically friendly buildings, this technology holds a lot of potential for the future of sustainable construction.

Sustainable House – Sydney, Australia

One person can make a difference. The Sustainable House in Sydney, Australia is one of the most notable instances of regenerative architecture. This house uses a rainwater collection system and solar panels to run completely off the grid. The home uses passive design, which minimizes the need for artificial lighting, heating, and cooling by orienting the structure to maximize natural light and airflow.

In addition, the Sustainable House makes use of greywater recycling, composting toilets, and low-impact building materials, including locally quarried stone and reclaimed wood. It proves that leading a sustainable lifestyle need not sacrifice style or comfort. Rather, it demonstrates how environmentally conscious architecture can provide stunning, eco-friendly homes that also improve the environment.

Benefits of Sustainable Buildings

Sustainable buildings provide numerous advantages to both the occupants and the environment. Among the principal advantages are:

Energy Efficiency: Energy-efficient features like energy-saving appliances, and renewable energy sources like solar or wind power are all part of the regenerative building design, which aim to reduce energy usage.

Better Health and Well-Being: Human health is taken into consideration when designing these structures. Better indoor air quality, natural light, and non-toxic materials make for healthier interior spaces, which lower the risk of respiratory ailments and enhance mental well-being.

Water Conservation: Sustainable buildings drastically cut down on water waste and consumption by utilizing water-saving technology, including rainwater harvesting, low-flow fixtures, and greywater recycling.

Environmental Impact: These structures actively aid in the restoration of natural ecosystems, going above and beyond merely minimizing harm. Regenerating natural resources, enhancing biodiversity, and addressing climate change are all aided by green walls and roofs, urban gardens, and sustainable building materials.

Financial Savings: Although regenerative buildings may require a larger initial investment, they are a wise financial decision over time due to the long-term reduction in energy and water use as well as lower maintenance expenses.

THE FUTURE OF SUSTAINABLE ARCHITECTURE

The move toward sustainable architecture heralds a new age in building, one in which structures serve as tools for mending the environment. Architects, builders, and engineers are extending the limits of what is feasible by merging state-of-the-art technologies with traditional, environmentally conscious building methods.

As we look to the future, we should anticipate an increasing number of structures that serve the requirements of both the environment and their residents. Sustainable structures will increase biodiversity, capture renewable energy, and improve community well-being. They will act as role models for endurance and maintenance, proving that we can develop for the future without endangering the condition of the environment.

BUILDING A REGENERATIVE FUTURE

Regenerative structures are clearing the way for a more sustainable and environmentally friendly future as the construction industry continues to change. We can shift the built environment from one that depletes resources to one that regenerates them by embracing energy-efficient designs, using new materials, and implementing green construction practices.

This new way of thinking aims to create environments that heal, replenish, and nourish the Earth and its inhabitants. Private sector planners are adopting these methods in more communities each year. Regenerative architecture is essential to creating a sustainable future in which people coexist peacefully with the environment as we continue to progress.

We assume responsibility for the future and contribute to the health and vitality of our planet by daring to adapt our built environments. By doing so, we make sure that future generations inherit a more resilient, sustainable, and regenerative world.

How can we shift our daily actions and perspectives to envision sustainable solutions for buildings?

CHAPTER 12

Clean Transportation

"Environmentally friendly cars will soon cease to be an option... they will become a necessity."

FUJO CHO, PRESIDENT
President of Toyota Motors

Humans are the species on the planet that have a special ability to modify their surroundings. Using our ability to take resources from the environment and then alter them to suit a new purpose, we have built a setting that supports a more comfortable way of living. We have also made many things that, while great ideas, have so far created problems for the planet. Fossil fuel automobiles are one such example. With the current state of knowledge, we have some choices for alternatives. Electric vehicles (EVs) are currently at the forefront, with hydrogen powered vehicles getting a lot of attention as well.

While we are at this point in our evolutionary understanding of energy potentials right now, I believe that there will be other advances that are currently just ideas (quantum energy, for instance). New developments will revolutionize our ability to travel, both on this planet and potentially allow interplanetary, or interstellar travel. Look at some of the work being done by the International Space Federation, led by Nassim Haramein.

The United States has done a poor job of creating an infrastructure that supports human transportation throughout the country other than by automobile. A few busses run, but even in metropolitan areas they are often unreliable or not timely. Many other countries have developed rail systems that enable travel that is convenient and timely, which can reduce the necessity for automobiles. One potential option that could make the U.S. a model for the future would be to build a hyperloop system. This could start with following the interstate system, and then build out to more remote communities. Building out our infrastructure with something like the hyperloop would also be a big boost to the economy as the building of the interstate system was in the 1950's.

Electric vehicles are leading the transportation revolution in the face of pollution, climate change, and the depletion of fossil resources. Rather than merely a change in technology they signify a broader movement toward sustainable solutions that balance environmental health and human advancement. From automobiles to boats to airplanes, electric mobility holds the potential of cutting emissions, enhancing air quality, and advancing humankind toward a day when mobility is not at the expense of the health of the planet.

This chapter explores the world of EVs, along with potential hydrogen vehicles, looking at developments in cars, boats, and airplanes. It also highlights important figures in the industry and the significant environmental advantages of this revolutionary change.

I have not yet purchased an all-electric vehicle. I have purchased a hybrid that we put 288,000+ miles on before letting it go as it started using oil. While we had to replace the main hybrid battery at around 210.000 miles, which cost of approximately $3,000, it was a great vehicle and led us to purchase another used hybrid. One of the downsides of any internal combustion vehicle is the maintenance required to keep them in working order. Electric vehicles in general require minimal maintenance, so the expense over time is reduced. EVs are only one potential solution, among other options for a healthier environment. There are hydrogen vehicles being developed that show a lot of promise. I also believe that there will be greater use of public transportation with many versatile solutions, thus reducing the need for personal vehicles. Again, an infrastructure upgrade with mass transit high-speed systems could be a key element in reducing pollution, while facilitating convenience.

Electric Autos: *Leading the Charge*

The electric vehicle revolution is most evident in automobiles, and some businesses are pushing the limits of what EVs can accomplish in terms of performance, sustainability, and range. Manufacturers that are advancing electric mobility, such as Tesla, Mercedes Electric, Ford Electric, and others, are at the forefront of this industry.

> *Tesla:* The electric vehicle movement has come to be associated with Elon Musk's company. Powered solely by electric batteries, Tesla automobiles are renowned for their exceptional range and rapid acceleration. For the average motorist, switching to electric cars has become easier thanks to Tesla's Supercharger network, which permits fast recharging and long-distance travel. In terms of luxury and convenience, electric automobiles may easily replace gasoline-powered vehicles while having a less environmental impact. Tesla's Model S, Model 3, Model X, and Model Y are just a few examples.

Mercedes Electric: With its all-electric EQ line, Mercedes-Benz is revolutionizing its brand. Elegance, range, and state-of-the-art technology are all embodied in the Mercedes EQS, a premium electric sedan. It is a reflection of the company's dedication to building cars that preserve luxury and performance while promoting environmental responsibility.

Ford Electric: The legendary F-150 Lightning truck and the Mustang Mach-E are Ford's entry into the electric vehicle industry. Ford is a well-known automaker. These vehicles demonstrate that EVs are useful for more than just commuting in cities; they can also be strong work-horses that can manage difficult tasks and long distances.

Kia, Hyundai, Honda, Toyota, Audi, VW, BMW, General Motors, Lucid, Nissan, Polestar, Rivian, and Volvo, are other companies that are also manufacturing EV's. So as we can see there is a growing interest in transitioning to electric driven options.

Plug-In America is a prominent advocacy group that promotes the increased use of EVs. It helps to facilitate the transition from internal combustion engines to cleaner, quieter, and more efficient EVs by offering support and educational materials to consumers who are interested in making the switch to electric vehicles.

Companies and media sources such as the *Electrek* Newsletter, which informs fans and customers on the most recent developments, legislative shifts, and improvements in electric mobility, are driving the greater EV movement. The transition to EVs is about building a more flexible and robust transportation system for the future, not only about sustainability.

Electric Boats: *Sailing Toward a Cleaner Future*

The electrification of maritime transport is just as critical as land-based vehicles. Boats and ships contribute significantly to global emissions, and electrification offers a pathway to reducing the pollution that affects both air quality and marine ecosystems. Companies are now leading the charge in developing electric boats that combine performance, range, and eco-friendliness.

Correct Craft Ski Nautique E: The Ski Nautique E from Correct Craft is an example of how electric power can be used in sports and leisure boats. It delivers the same thrilling experience of water skiing but without the carbon emissions and noise pollution associated with traditional gas-powered engines. Being a water skier, I became concerned about the pollution from gas-powered boats, it was exciting to see this possible alternative developed.

Elco Motor Yachts: With a variety of electric propulsion systems for boats, Elco is one of the pioneers in the electric boating industry. To lessen the negative environmental effects of boating, they offer options for both new construction and the retrofitting of conventional boats with electric motors.

Axopar Boats: The Finnish boat maker Axopar is developing models of both fully electric and hybrid boats. These boats are made to function in delicate marine habitats, such as protected seas and national parks, where keeping emissions and noise levels to a minimum is essential to protecting native species.

As technology advances, we should anticipate seeing more electric options for ferries, fishing boats, and even larger vessels that go through commercial shipping lanes. Electric boats are already more widely available. We will experience cleaner rivers and a decrease in marine pollution with the implementation of these advancements.

Electric Aircraft: *The Future of Aviation*
Not only can electric power be used on land or at sea, but entrepreneurs are currently attempting to take electric power into the air. One of the industries with the highest global carbon emissions is aviation. By significantly lowering the carbon impact of air travel and providing quieter, more efficient flights, electric aircraft have the potential to completely transform the aviation sector.

e-Genius: A fully electric aircraft intended for training and short-range flying developed by the University of Stuttgart. It has demonstrated that significant flying durations with reduced emissions are possible with electric aircraft. As battery technology advances, e-Genius-style aircraft may soon be a regular sight at local airports all over the world.

Black Kestrel: By creating an aircraft with a longer range, Black Kestrel is expanding the possibilities for electric flight. Its modern styling and cutting-edge battery technology demonstrate how electric aviation has the potential to displace conventional fuel-powered aircraft on short-haul flights.

magniX: Offering electric propulsion systems for aircraft, magniX is a frontrunner in the electric aviation sector. To lower the expenses and lessen the environmental effects of regional air travel, they have already started testing electric aircraft for use in the commercial market.

Diamond Aircraft: An established participant in the aviation sector, Diamond Aircraft has embraced electric propulsion by creating electric training aircraft that enable pilots to hone their skills in a more sustainable, quiet, and clean manner. Their work in creating electric airplanes is facilitating more accessible and environmentally friendly flight instruction.

Joby, Yuneec, Ametek, Thales, Safran, BAE Systems, Honeywell, Airbus, RTX, Boeing, are other companies that are also developing electric options for air transportation.

Although there is still a long way to go before aviation is fully electrified, the initial progress is encouraging. We may soon witness a time when air travel is no longer associated with environmental harm due to these advancements in battery technology and electric infrastructure. Electric aircraft have the potential to usher in a new era of economical, quiet, and environmentally friendly aviation.

THE ENVIRONMENTAL BENEFITS OF ELECTRIC VEHICLES

There are many environmental benefits associated with EVs. Replacing internal combustion engines with electric motors can greatly reduce greenhouse gas emissions, air pollution, and our dependency on fossil fuels. Here are a few of the main advantages:

Decrease in Greenhouse Gas Emissions: Since EVs don't emit any tailpipe emissions, the amount of carbon dioxide, one of the primary drivers of climate change, is significantly reduced. Research indicates that even after taking the electricity required for EV charging into consideration, electric automobiles still have a much smaller carbon footprint than cars that run on gasoline.

Better Air Quality: Electric vehicles, especially in metropolitan areas, help to create cleaner air because they don't release pollutants like nitrogen oxides and particulate matter. A healthier population and fewer respiratory problems may result from this.

Renewable Energy Integration: Clean energy may power EVs as the world moves toward renewable energy sources like solar and wind. Our energy and environment problems can be effectively solved by combining renewable energy with EVs.

Energy Efficiency: Compared to internal combustion engines, electric motors have a considerably higher energy efficiency. Electric motors may drive the wheels with 80–90% of the energy from the battery, but gas engines usually only convert 20–30% of the energy in gasoline into motion. Because of their efficiency, EVs are a better option for energy conservation.

THE ROAD AHEAD: CHALLENGES AND OPPORTUNITIES

The switch to EVs is not without its difficulties, despite the fact that they provide many advantages. Important problems that still need to be solved include range anxiety, battery production, and charging infrastructure. But these challenges are gradually being overcome by improvements in infrastructure and technological advancements.

Governments and businesses are making significant investments in the construction of charging stations as part of their efforts to make EVs as convenient to fuel as conventional cars. The field of battery technology is also developing quickly. Solid-state battery advancements promise increased safety, quicker charging times, and longer battery lives.

Furthermore, the circular economy approach to battery production—which recycles and reuses resources from old batteries—will help guarantee the long-term switch to electric vehicles is sustainable.

Hydrogen Alternatives: *A Potential Future for Clean Energy* As a clean, effective, and adaptable energy source, hydrogen fuel offers a strong case for minimizing dependency on fossil fuels. Hydrogen is the most prevalent element in the universe and has a wide range of uses, such as energy storage, industrial processes, and transportation. For example, cars that run on hydrogen only release water vapor, which makes them a green choice that supports international sustainability objectives. Moreover, because of its high energy density, hydrogen is especially useful for heavy-duty vehicles like trucks, trains, and ships, where electric alternatives are limited.

Hydrogen power holds enormous promise, but it also faces several obstacles, chief among them being a lack of infrastructure for its effective production, storage, and distribution. The current cost of producing hydrogen and its frequent reliance on fossil fuels may outweigh its environmental benefits. Despite being a potential alternative, green hydrogen produced with renewable energy is still prohibitively expensive because electrolyzers and renewable power demand large capital investments. Furthermore, because of its low volumetric energy density, hydrogen presents technical hurdles for storage and transportation, requiring sophisticated solutions like cryogenic storage or high-pressure tanks.

Governments, businesses, and researchers must work together to address these issues by making investments in infrastructure, developing affordable technology, and drafting supportive legislation. Hydrogen as a clean energy option could be crucial in decarbonizing industries where electrification is less practical as the infrastructure grows and costs come down. This would be a big step toward a robust and sustainable energy future.

Personal Rapid Transit

One innovative idea for sustainable urban travel is Personal Rapid Transit (PRT). The goal of the planned system is to create a network of self-sufficient, electric pods that operate on raised walkways, providing quick, effective, and emission-free transportation throughout communities such as Milpitas, California. PRT systems, in contrast to traditional mass transportation, improve last-mile connectivity and cut down on wait times, which makes them perfect for cities that are dealing with carbon emissions and traffic. PRT projects provide examples of how small-scale, modular transportation might be expanded to satisfy 21st-century mobility demands while reducing environmental impact by combining smart infrastructure and renewable energy.

THE FUTURE OF TRANSPORTATION

Transportation electrification is not merely a fad; rather, it is an important step toward building a world that is resilient, sustainable, and environmentally conscientious. Electric vehicles are changing the way we travel, lessening our impact on the environment, and opening the door to a time when transportation coexists with the environment, whether on land, at sea, or in the air.

The path ahead is hopeful. As we dare to transform our transportation networks, electric cars will be needed to cut emissions, enhance air quality, and face the urgent issue of climate change. Choosing electric transportation is about more than implementing new technology, it means rethinking our relationship with the environment and our duty to future generations. The electric car revolution will quicken with sustained innovation, funding, and public backing, bringing us one step closer to a future in which everyone has access to efficient, quiet, and clean transportation.

There are groups still working on additional alternatives, for example, hydrogen vehicles, have shown some promise. However, at this time, EVs are making the most progress toward a better environment. It should be noted that in places like the United States that rely heavily on personal vehicles, there are several opportunities for evolving our infrastructure. Better local low-emission transportation systems, as well as high-speed long-distance ground transportation, across the country, could have a significant reduction on the need for personal vehicles and airplanes.

How can we shift our daily actions and perspectives to contemplate sustainable solutions for transportation?

"Renewable energy could reduce emissions but also create jobs and improve public health."

~ PAUL POLMAN

CHAPTER 13

Energy

O ur capacity to shift from a society that depends on fossil fuels to one that welcomes renewable energy will determine the future of our planet. Renewable energy is currently the most practical and long-term answer as we face the realities of climate change, depletion of natural resources, and rising demand for energy. Using the sun, wind, water, and geothermal heat that the Earth naturally possesses, renewable energy methods provide electricity without consuming limited resources or negatively affecting the environment. Again, it is noteworthy to mention the work being done at the International Space Federation on new potential energy systems. While I desire to move from fossil fuels to renewable alternatives, I am also realistic in that it will take a considerable amount of time to extricate ourselves from the infrastructure around this industry.

The main features of renewable energy are examined next, with special attention paid to the functions of solar, wind, and wave energy. Additionally, this section highlights many of the companies and technological advancements spearheading the world's shift to cleaner, greener energy sources.

The home we are currently occupying produces over 90% of our electricity from solar. Between the garage and house roofs, there are 36 panels.

The pressing need to lessen our dependency on fossil fuels is at the heart of the renewable energy movement. For a very long time, the main energy sources for industry, transportation, and the production of electricity have been coal, oil, and natural gas. Unfortunately, the main greenhouse gas causing global warming, carbon dioxide, is released in large quantities when fossil fuels are burned. Fossil fuels not only contribute to climate change but also contaminate the air, water, and land, endangering ecosystems and public health.

Making the switch to renewable energy is important for lowering the consumption of fossil fuels and lessening the potential harm these traditional energy sources have on the environment. In contrast, renewable energy sources are plentiful, clean, and replenished spontaneously. These renewable resources can be converted into power without emitting harmful pollutants thanks to technologies like solar panels and wind turbines.

SOLAR ENERGY

One of the most prevalent and easily accessible renewable energy sources on Earth is solar energy. If we can effectively harness it, the Sun's energy can power the Earth several times over. Solar panels often contain photovoltaic cells, which are used to convert sunlight into electricity.

Solar technology is now more accessible, economical, and efficient than it has ever been, thanks to recent developments. Solar panels are being incorporated into windows automobiles, and rooftops as well as enormous solar farms. In addition to being a sustainable energy source, solar energy gives towns, businesses, and homes greater energy independence.

The use of solar energy is being spearheaded by a number of programs and organizations:

Rocky Mountain Institute (RMI): The RMI is a pioneer in the promotion of solar energy and other renewable energy sources. Their research highlights how crucial it is to move away from fossil fuels and toward greener energy options to lower carbon emissions.

The Third Industrial Revolution: To characterize the worldwide transition to renewable energy, economist and proponent of sustainability Jeremy Rifkin invented the phrase "The Third Industrial Revolution." According to his vision, decentralized technologies that enable individuals and groups to generate their own power using solar energy play a crucial part in democratizing energy.

The National Renewable Energy Laboratory (NREL) is a leading research organization in solar energy, spearheading advancements in solar panel efficiency, storage solutions, and solar grid integration. Their efforts are essential to scaling up solar energy and establishing it as the main energy source for the next generations.

WIND ENERGY

Another important component of the renewable energy scene is wind energy, which uses turbines to transform the kinetic energy of the wind into electrical power. Because wind power is scalable and can be built in both large offshore arrays and small, localized farms, it is an especially appealing energy source.

Around the world, wind farms are proliferating, with the United States, Germany, and Denmark spearheading the trend. Because offshore wind can capture stronger, more consistent winds over the ocean, it has become increasingly popular.

Global Wind Energy Council (GWEC): The GWEC is committed to advancing wind energy as a vital component of solving the world's energy problems. They collaborate with corporations, governments, and other relevant parties to increase wind energy capacity and advance laws that support its expansion.

WAVE ENERGY

One of the most promising, yet little-used, renewable energy sources is wave energy. Since the oceans, make up over 70% of the planet's surface, wave energy has the potential to be a consistent and dependable power source. Wave power systems are an environmentally friendly way to create electricity by harnessing the energy of ocean waves.

Wave potential is a near relative of wind energy. Wave power converts the energy of the waves in the ocean into electrical power. Wave energy is still in its infancy, but it has great promise for areas with long coastlines. By offering a consistent and reliable supply of renewable energy, this technology may be used in conjunction with solar and wind power.

The European Marine Energy Centre (EMEC): The EMEC is dedicated to the advancement of technology related to tidal and wave energy. Their testing and research facilities are assisting in the development of workable methods for utilizing ocean generated electricity.

The predictability of wave energy is one of its main benefits. In contrast to solar and wind power, which are reliant on the weather, wave patterns are relatively stable and are highly forecastable. Because of this, wave energy is a desirable alternative for coastal areas where it may supplement other renewable energy sources.

Businesses and organizations are funding the advancement of wave energy technologies. Wave energy has a lot of potential to contribute to the world's renewable energy mix in the future, even though it is still currently in the early stages of commercialization.

SMART GRIDS

The difficulty of incorporating variable energy sources like solar, wind, and wave power into the electrical grid needs to be solved as these renewable energy sources proliferate. A smart grid is an updated electrical system that makes use of digital technology to track and regulate energy flow in order to guarantee dependable and efficient delivery of power.

Maximizing the use of renewable energy requires smart grids. They provide a better energy supply and help coordinate demand. Additionally, demand response systems let users take part in energy management by storing or redirecting excess renewable energy.

Advanced batteries and other energy storage technologies are essential to the integration of renewable energy sources. By allowing excess energy from renewable sources to be stored for later use, energy storage helps mitigate supply variations to maintain a steady and uninterrupted power supply.

RENEWABLE SUPPORT

The switch to renewable energy involves more than simply technological advancements; it also calls for investment, supportive legislation, and regulatory environments. International organizations, corporations, and governments are collaborating to hasten the adoption of renewable energy technology and establish the prerequisites for their success.

UN Global Compact: This initiative urges companies all around the world to embrace socially conscious and sustainable business practices, such as switching to renewable energy. Businesses that ratify the compact pledge to invest in renewable energy sources and lessen their carbon footprints.

Green New Deal: The United States proposed legislative framework seeks to solve economic injustice and climate change by investing in renewable energy, phasing out fossil fuels, and creating green jobs. It reflects the rising understanding that renewable energy offers both environmental and financial benefits.

Sunrise Movement: This youth-led group promotes climate justice and sustainable energy sources. Their grassroots initiatives seek to mobilize political action in support of the clean energy transition and increase public awareness of its necessity.

Making the switch to renewable energy also offers major financial advantages. Renewable energy is becoming more affordable relative to fossil fuels as its costs continue to decline. Investing in renewable energy lowers the financial risks related to fluctuating fossil fuel costs while also generating jobs in production, installation, and maintenance.

Projects using renewable energy also have the potential to stimulate their local economies, especially in underserved and rural areas. For instance, wind and solar farms can give farmers and landowners a new source of revenue, while local businesses profit from the increase in investment and jobs.

Renewable energy is our future; it is no longer a pipe dream. It is becoming the cheapest per kWh and in February of 2024 the United States produced 21.4% of its electricity from renewables. The likelihood that clean, renewable energy sources will power the world is growing thanks to innovations like energy storage and smart grids, as well as energy sources like solar, wind, and wave power. We safeguard the environment and build a more robust, sustainable, and just global economy as we lessen our reliance on fossil fuels.

There is no doubt that the future of energy is renewable, but getting there will take courage, ingenuity, and teamwork. To expedite the shift to clean energy and guarantee that future generations inherit a planet that is healthy and sustainable, firms, individuals, and governments all have a part to play.

We embrace renewable energy as a chance to rethink our relationship with the world and as a means of addressing the environmental issues we face today in our adventurous evolution. We can fuel a future that is more equitable, cleaner, and greener for everyone by using renewable energy.

How can we shift our daily actions and perspectives to ponder sustainable solutions for energy?

"We don't need a handful of people doing zero waste perfectly. We need millions of people doing it imperfectly."

~ ANNE MARIE BONNEAU
Reducing the Footprint, Reimagining Waste

CHAPTER 14

Zero Waste

The push for zero waste signifies a profound change in our perspectives on sustainability, disposal, and consumption. Fundamentally, zero waste involves reevaluating how we use materials and products throughout their whole lifecycle, from their initial design, manufacture, and consumption to their eventual recycling and reintegration back into the environment. The objective is to reduce, if not completely eliminate, the amount of garbage sent to landfills and incinerators to protect the environment and conserve resources.

It takes a shift in broader systemic structures as well as individual habits to implement a zero-waste approach. It's about viewing trash as an issue that can be solved rather than an unavoidable part of contemporary life. As we advance in this field, we must have the vision to see a time in which resources are only reutilized rather than waste.

One reason for coming to terms with our waste issues is how it affects our health. An article in *Integrative Medicine: A Clinicians Journal* from September 2024 illustrates this issue. The article 'Impact of Microplastics and Nanoplastics on Human Health," by authors Lyn Patrick, ND, and Joseph Pizzorno, ND, indicates how these plastics can affect the heart, bowel, and liver. It highlights why we need to reduce the amount of plastic we use in all areas and control the waste from that use.

What is Zero Waste?

A set of guidelines known as zero waste encourages restructuring resource life cycles to maximize product reuse and reduce waste. The intention is to avoid sending any waste to the ocean, incinerators, or landfills. Rather, the things we use on a daily basis ought to be considered resources that can be returned to the ecosystem. Rethinking how we consume and how businesses manufacture things is part of this approach; circular economies are preferred over the traditional "take, make, dispose" paradigm.

The Zero Waste International Alliance promotes the conservation of all resources via responsible production, consumption, recycling, and reuse of goods, materials, and packaging. This is a systemic shift that affects everything from daily routines in the home to corporate regulations.

The Impact of Waste on the Planet

The quantity of rubbish created annually on a global scale keeps increasing. The World Bank estimates that at least 33% of the 2.01 billion tons of municipal solid garbage produced worldwide each year is not managed in a way that is safe for the environment. Landfills release methane, a powerful gas that warms the planet, which is one of the main greenhouse gas emissions they produce. With over 8 million tons of plastic garbage poured into the oceans annually, ocean pollution from plastic trash also poses a threat to marine ecosystems.

Humans take the equivalent of a credit card worth of plastic into their bodies each week. The scientific Journal *Nature* announced a landmark study in March of 2024 that links microplastics to serious health problems.

Waste has an unsustainable negative environmental impact, both in terms of pollution and the resources needed to make throwaway goods. The zero-waste movement tackles the resource and environmental issues, which is why it is so essential to building a sustainable future.

ZeroWaste.Org: A Global Movement for Change

One of the main groups spearheading the global Zero Waste movement is ZeroWaste.Org. They give people, companies, and communities a foundation for making the switch to a zero-waste way of living. Their efforts are concentrated on lowering the amount of garbage produced, enhancing waste management techniques, sand promoting laws that encourage waste reduction.

ZeroWaste.Org works with businesses and governments to achieve quantifiable reductions in waste transported to landfills through their certification programs. Their objective is to establish a circular economy that prioritizes the continuous reuse of materials above their disposal by promoting the redesign of products and systems.

Zero Waste Home: A Model for Personal Responsibility

The concept of living waste-free on a personal level has gained popularity thanks to Bea Johnson's *Zero Waste Home* movement. Johnson's family of four follows the "5 Rs" of zero rubbish: Refuse, Reduce, Reuse, Recycle, and Rot (compost); as a result, they only generate a tiny jar of rubbish a year.

Reducing personal waste begins with refusing needless things, such as single-use plastics, which is possibly the most crucial step in the process. The movement places a strong emphasis on conscious consumerism, advising people to choose durable and reusable products and only purchase what they truly need.

A growing number of people are being motivated to live more simply, consume less, and accept accountability for their waste output by Zero Waste Home. This is consistent with the larger cultural trend toward minimalism, which prioritizes experiences over material belongings and quality over quantity.

Zero Waste Europe: *Advocating for Systemic Change*
At the policy level, Zero Waste Europe collaborates with governments and businesses throughout the continent to put policies supporting zero-waste practices into effect. This comprises laws designed to lessen the manufacturing of plastics, enhance recycling programs, and motivate companies to use the circular economy.

Extended Producer Responsibility (EPR) is a policy strategy that holds producers accountable for the lifecycle of their products, from design to disposal, and is strongly supported by Zero Waste Europe. The EPR regulations encourage businesses to create products with less of an impact on the environment that are simpler to discard or reuse.

Zero Waste Europe advocates for systemic reforms that can drastically lower the quantity of garbage that ends up in landfills and the ocean. Some of these improvements include the ban on single-use plastics and the betterment of recycling infrastructure.

WasteZero Solutions: *Bridging the Gap for Municipalities*
WasteZero Solutions works in partnership with US towns to assist them in achieving zero waste objectives. WasteZero helps communities in implementing workable solutions that

decrease the amount of garbage transported to landfills while increasing recycling and composting rates.

Pay-As-You-Throw (PAYT) systems, which tax households for the waste they produce while offering free or significantly discounted recycling services, are among the policies that WasteZero supports. These initiatives provide a straightforward yet efficient means of cutting trash on a big scale—they have been shown to reduce waste by up to 50% in participating communities.

Zero Emissions Research and Initiatives: *Innovating Toward Zero Waste*

The goal of Zero Emissions Research and Initiatives (ZERI) is to develop novel approaches to address environmental problems, such as waste management. Notably ZERI's methodology places a strong emphasis on integrating many fields to create sustainable systems that resemble natural processes.

For example, ZERI supports biogas systems, which produce compost as a byproduct and turn organic waste into electricity. This produces useful agricultural inputs and renewable energy in addition to reducing waste. Their work emphasizes how crucial it is to create waste management plans that both solve the issue of trash and benefit the environment.

Companies Repackaging for Lower Waste

Many businesses are reconsidering how they package their goods in an effort to cut waste, gravitating toward environmentally friendly options that have the least negative effects. This emphasizes using reusable containers, cutting back on single-use plastics, and switching to packaging materials that can be composted or biodegraded.

Loop, a global reuse platform, is leading the way in a circular packaging strategy that allows consumers to return empty containers for cleaning, refilling, and reuse. By working with Loop, well-known companies like Procter & Gamble, Nestlé, and Unilever are able to provide their products in robust, reusable containers, significantly reducing the amount of plastic trash produced.

A Chilean startup called Algramo is redefining packaging by providing household goods in clever, reusable containers. Customers refill their containers at vending stations, paying by weight and purchasing only what they need. This creative method minimizes excess by encouraging a pay-for-what-you-use model and reducing packaging waste.

Another pioneer in waste minimization is Lush Cosmetics, which sells "naked" goods—products with no packaging at all. Their solid soaps, shampoos, and conditioners do away with the need for plastic bottles, and even the materials in their wrapped items are compostable and biodegradable.

Businesses such as these are not only cutting waste but also establishing new benchmarks for sustainability in the sector by repackaging their products. They take us one step closer to a world with zero waste by showing that waste can be reduced with innovation and creative thinking, and without compromising convenience or product quality.

Down to Earth (Netflix): *Documenting Sustainability with Example for Zero Waste*

Actor Zac Efron stars in the Netflix documentary series Down to Earth, which explores global attempts to transition to sustainability, including zero waste programs. The series features groups and individuals that are setting the standard for cutting-edge resource conservation and waste reduction.

Down to Earth offers a positive outlook on a more sustainable future while drawing attention to the urgent need for international action on trash reduction through the use of real-world examples. It challenges viewers to consider their personal waste practices and motivates them to move toward a zero-waste way of living.

futurefoodsystem: *Designing Waste-Free Living*

The futurefoodsystem project shows how a completely self-sufficient house can operate waste-free. This closed-loop home, designed by environmentalist Joost Bakker, demonstrates how homes may reduce waste through intelligent design and interconnected systems to grow its own food, recycle its garbage, and produce all of its own energy. Waste is converted into a resource via Bakker's approach. Water is collected and reused, while food leftovers produce compost, which grows more food. This model shows that zero waste is not just an ideal but also a real possibility and offers a guide for designing sustainable homes of the future.

Repair and Mending Movements

Movements for repair and mending have emerged as crucial allies in the fight for a future with zero waste. These programs enable people to repair broken products rather than throw them away, prolonging their useful lives and cutting down on landfill trash. The Netherlands-based Repair Café Foundation has assisted in the establishment of hundreds of neighborhood repair cafés worldwide, where volunteers fix everything from garments to appliances (Repair Café, n.d.). To help people disassemble and fix their own broken things, the Fixit Clinic organizes pop-up repair sessions at libraries and schools around the United States (Fixit Clinic, 2023). By encouraging consumers to fix and resell their equipment, Patagonia's Worn Wear program transforms a business strategy into a sustainable philosophy (Patagonia, 2023). The cultural change from consumer disposability to collective care and stewardship is exemplified by these examples. These efforts remind us that fixing things is a step toward mending the earth by prioritizing repair over replacement.

Reimagining Waste: *The Future of Zero Waste*
Beyond lowering the quantity of waste, we produce, zero waste aims to radically alter our relationship with the planet's resources. We can design systems and products that extend the life of materials, by moving toward a circular economy, cutting down on waste and the demand for virgin resources.

The movement is gaining traction as more towns, companies, and people adopt zero waste policies. It forces us to reconsider not just how we handle trash but also how our entire economic structure is built. In order to progress toward a waste-free world, we must be creative, cooperative, and courageous enough to change our systems for the good of coming generations.

We welcome the prospect of a society in which materials are used continuously and waste is nonexistent, enabling a sustainable and regenerative future for everybody, by taking the risk to evolve our thinking.

How will you adjust your mindset to reflect on sustainable solutions for zero waste?

CHAPTER 15

Reimagine Economy

"We seem to be in a time where innovation and critical thinking are energizing a new economic paradigm. One that encourages a sustainable future. YES!"

~ Unknown

We have evolved our society around an economy that leaves us in a place of unequal resource availability. How do we build an economy in which every person has the ability to support themselves and their family with opportunities for growth and only a reasonable amount of time expended? We need to look at how our universe works, with each piece contributing and receiving in ways that support both the whole and the individual. It is time for our species to realize that we cannot be our best until everyone is their best.

To paraphrase Martin Luther King Jr.:

"All life is interrelated. We are caught in an inescapable network of mutuality, tied in a single garment of destiny. <u>Whatever affects one directly, affects all indirectly.</u> As long as there is poverty in this world, no one can be totally rich even if they have a billion dollars. As long as diseases are rampant and millions of people cannot expect to live more than twenty or thirty years, no one can be totally healthy, even if they just got a clean bill of health from the finest clinic in America. We are so interrelated that I can never be all that I ought to be until you are all that you ought to be. And, you can never be all that you ought to be until I am all that I ought to be."

The economy is dynamic, just like any other living system. It changes as a result of the needs, objectives, and values of those who take part in it. To address the problems posed by the impending environmental, social, and technological transformations, we need to rethink the way our economy is structured. To achieve a more sustainable and inclusive future, we must investigate several economic models, each with its own benefits and challenges.

Free Market Economy

The foundation of the free market economy is the idea that people can exchange products and services freely and so generate wealth as a group, all while acting in their own best interests. In this system, innovation flourishes as companies strive to satisfy customer needs in novel and effective ways.

Benefits:

- Promotes entrepreneurship and creativity, which propels technological advancements in fields like green and clean energy.
- Provides flexibility, enabling markets to quickly adjust to changing consumer preferences, trends, and resource availability.
- As businesses compete to win over customers who are becoming more environmentally concerned, they may produce more environmentally friendly products.
- Self-regulation—prices adjust based on demand.
- Incentivized productivity—people and businesses work harder.

Challenges:
- Market forces have the power to put profit ahead of social and environmental welfare in the absence of appropriate regulation.
- Emphasis on short-term financial benefit may jeopardize long-term sustainability initiatives especially in sectors such as fossil fuel and resource extraction.
- Certain people may become increasingly excluded from the advantages of innovation and clean technology as a result of growing economic disparity.
- Income inequality—wealth concentration.
- Exploitation & ethical concerns—pursuit of profit.
- Economic instability—booms and busts can occur without regulation.

The free market may drive sustainable solutions in this new economic paradigm, provided it is tempered with sensible regulation that encourages innovation without endangering the health of the environment.

Command Economy

Resources can be swiftly mobilized in a command economy, where distribution and production are managed centrally, to meet pressing societal requirements. Theoretically, command economies may adopt sustainable policies that give top priority to equal resource distribution and environmental protection.

Benefits:
- Centralized control makes long-term planning possible, which facilitates the implementation of

significant sustainability projects like infrastructure for renewable energy sources or universal access to clean water.

- Environmental and social responsibility in industry operations can be enhanced by government oversight.
- Inequality can be decreased by guaranteeing necessities like clean energy, healthcare, education and income.

Challenges:

- Insufficient competition can hinder innovation, resulting in ineffectiveness of research and development which delays uptake of novel technology.
- Rigid. centralized economies can find it challenging to adjust to sudden shifts in consumer preferences or technological breakthroughs.
- The presence of corruption or inefficiency in the bureaucracy could compromise the overall efficacy of sustainability initiatives.
- Limited consumer choice.

Even if the command economy can give structure to long-term sustainability goals, it is less flexible and innovative, which makes it less able to keep up with the rapid changes in the modern economy.

Mixed Economy

A command economy's monitoring and the creativity of the free market are balanced by the mixed economy. In order to correct market imperfections and work towards fair resource allocation, a mixed economic model combines government control with the freedom for private ownership and business.

Benefits:
- Combines the market's efficiency with the regulatory control required to empower social justice and environmental sustainability.
- Government intervention through the imposition of taxes, subsidies, or restrictions can address market failures such as pollution and resource overconsumption.
- In sectors such as waste management, transportation, and renewable energy, public-private partnerships can stimulate innovation by utilizing both public funds and competitive market forces.

Challenges:
- It can be challenging to strike the correct balance between free enterprise and, regulation with too little allowing unchecked environmental deterioration and too much limiting innovation.
- Bureaucracy in mixed economies can cause decision-making to move slowly, especially in fields like technology that often change quickly.
- Market-based incentives might not always be in line with sustainability's long-term objectives, necessitating ongoing monitoring and adjustment.
- Mixed economies offer a tempting paradigm in an innovative environment. They encourage innovation in business by allowing for both growth and regulation within a framework that supports sustainability.

Subsidy Economy
Governments that support businesses or sectors that advance national or international sustainability goals—like

renewable energy, sustainable agriculture, or public trans-portation—get financial assistance in a subsidy economy.

Benefits:
- Focuses funding on sectors of the economy that, while still necessary for sustainability, may not be profitable on their own, such as carbon capture or renewable energy technologies.
- Encourages the use of renewable energy and other sustainable practices, which helps to ease the transition away from fossil fuels and other businesses that produce pollution.
- Lowers the risk for businesses creating expensive, high-impact inventions, promoting more audacious sustainability breakthroughs.

Challenges:
- If subsidies are not managed effectively or are provided to businesses that are no longer viable, they can cause market distortion and inefficiencies, such as continuous support for fossil fuel sectors.
- If sectors grow overly dependent on government assistance, it may eventually hinder competition and innovation.
- Political favoritism or improper funding distribution, where subsidies are given out in accordance with political agendas rather than real sustainability objectives, is a problem.
- Subsidies, according to this economic paradigm, are essential for hastening the shift to a sustainable future, but they must be handled cautiously to prevent inducing dependency or supporting outmoded businesses.

Socialist Economy

The goal of a socialist economy is to distribute wealth and resources more fairly among all citizens, so it places a strong emphasis on collective or governmental ownership of resources. This system has the capacity to put long-term resource management and sustainability ahead of immediate financial gain.

Benefits:

- Socialist economies can enable potential so that no one is left behind in the shift to a green economy by emphasizing sustainability and fair access to resources while concentrating on the common good.
- Comprehensive sustainability initiatives like universal healthcare, universal education, and universal access to renewable energy can be made possible by centralized planning.
- It is possible to manage wealth and resource distribution in a way that lessens income inequality and fosters social cohesion.

Challenges:

- A lack of market rivalry, can lead to inefficiency which can delay the adoption of novel technologies or creative approaches.
- If centralized control is not adequately regulated or monitored, it may result in corruption or poor management.
- There might be less motivation for product and service innovation and improvement in the absence of the free market's incentive systems.

The socialist economy presents a vision of long-term sustainability and fair resource allocation, but it poses difficulties for promoting innovation and market responsiveness in the face of quickly changing global demands.

Countries

Different economic systems give countries unique options for allocating resources, defining the role of the state, and organizing production. Many people point to the United States as a prime example of a free market economy, where supply and demand dominate pricing and private ownership and competition spur innovation (Heritage Foundation, 2023). On the opposite extreme, North Korea is an example of a command economy, where the government has almost complete authority over labor, production, and distribution, leaving little opportunity for private industry (CIA, 2024). Cuba is an example of a socialist economy, where the state owns and runs the means of production and economic planning prioritizes equality and the general welfare over private gain (Central Bank of Cuba, 2021).

An excellent example of a mixed economy is provided by Germany, which strikes a balance between free entrepreneurship, a substantial social safety net, and regulatory control to foster social justice and innovation (OECD, 2022). In the meantime, Saudi Arabia is a prime example of a subsidy economy, in which public funds, particularly those derived from oil, are utilized to fund extensive energy, housing, and social program subsidies, thereby influencing economic activity through financial inducements (World Bank, 2021). The various tactics governments employ to match economic results with political agendas and cultural norms are demonstrated by these five economic models.

A New Paradigm: *Energizing a Sustainable Future*

Diedre McCloskey PhD. and Hazel Henderson PhD. have both spoken on the topic of having ethics in congruence with the economy. I admire their thoughtful expression on this subject. Through continuous questioning and seeking balance toward a fair and equitable economy we might enable a future that respects natural resources and thus not damage a sustainable planet and the humans on it.

While I am not an economist and have to do research to understand most things, it is clear to me that there has been a significant shift in our economic structure since I was growing up in the 1950s. During the 50s, 60s, and somewhat in the 70s, it was normal for incomes to keep up with inflation. After the shift to shareholder equity in corporations, and tax cuts based on the theory of trickle-down economics, it was much harder for incomes to keep up. So, I would say it is time to move from an economy in favor of large corporations and those with the most wealth to one that is in favor of the planet and humanity.

A NOVEL APPROACH:
CREATING A VIBRANT FUTURE

Now is the time to make a bold move. No single economic model is perfect, but we can create a system that benefits people and the environment by combining the best features of all of them, whether it be the free market's entrepreneurial spirit, the command economy's long-term planning, or the socialist economy's equitable distribution. The fundamental assumptions behind our understanding of and behavior within economic systems are being transformed by the convergence of innovation and critical thinking.

In this new economic paradigm, regeneration is valued over exploitation, equity is valued over endless accumulation, and innovation is valued over stagnation. It dares to imagine a society in which all businesses, all governments, and all individuals realize that sustainable practices are essential to ensuring our shared future. A world in which the economy and environment coexist harmoniously.

We can build a more sustainable and balanced economy by encouraging private sector innovation, regulating markets to safeguard the environment, and supporting subsidies for green innovation. It's important to lay the groundwork for a prosperous, resilient, and sustainable future in addition to solving the issues of the past.

To adapt to a changing global environment, we must keep asking ourselves these and other important questions as we develop and adjust our economic systems. Realizing that the future is something we make together rather than something that happens to us is at the core of the *Dare to Evolve* philosophy.

How can we shift our daily actions and perspectives to consider impartial solutions for the economy?

Afterword

This has been a work of love. This is a project to provide information on resources for sustainable solutions that will enable the survival of humankind on this planet. With today's continual challenges we need to be able to distribute information regarding hopeful projects that will produce long-term solutions.

For what purpose has Mother Earth enabled me here at this time? Do I have the courage to give up my position on any given subject and relearn with an open mind and unconditional love?

Consciousness regarding regeneration with sustainability is increasing and there are more resources available that speak to cooperation, coordination, collaboration and reciprocity. It is an exciting time in which physics is now providing the proof that we can move forward with solutions that are in resonance with providing energy solutions that are clean instead of continuing our history of dissonance and pollution.

I have experienced various purposes in this life, many of them totally unconscious. At this time, I know my purpose is to share solutions that are leading us toward regenerating where needed, and enabling a sustainable future that will support life! We cannot sustain the status quo. Sustainability through regeneration is required to bring us back to what was truly sustainable before humans intervened in erroneous ways.

I love regeneration and sustainability. Our planet supports us with life in abundance. How do we maintain our responsibility to long-term survival of the eco-system? I hope to support a continuing evolution of being in balance with; whether it be our own personal issues, how we are treating each other, or how we treat Earth and all of our fellow species.

Resources

*"The throwing out of balance of the resources of nature
throws out of balance also the lives of men."*

~ Franklin D. Roosevelt

Not only must we take action, but knowledge is also essential on our path to a more sustainable and regenerative future: knowledge of the planet, our place in it, and the creative ideas that lead the way. A selection of materials that act as benchmarks for those who are willing to progress is provided in this appendix. All the references point to wisdom and action for a more hopeful and equitable future, acting as a guiding light.

Mirrors In The Earth

This book by Asia Suler was an inspiration. It has a message of how our planet enables a looking glass into those areas where we can see solutions for almost any problem. It tells the story of health recovery by working with the Earth, as well as how the various aspects of our planet support us in even subtle ways we still don't totally understand. Asia has a knack of wording truth so that it stands out, arouses our curiosity, and supports solutions that are often overlooked.

A Life on Our Planet

This film on Netflix, which features Sir David Attenborough as the narrator, gives an analysis of the significant shifts in Earth's biodiversity over the course of a lifetime. It is a message of hope as well as a sharp warning. The core ideas of this documentary are echoed by Attenborough's call for restorative practices, which emphasize how we protect ourselves by preserving the natural world. It pushes for a change from exploitation to regeneration in our interaction with the environment.

The Systems View of Life

Co-authored by Fritjof Capra and Pier Luigi Luisi, the book *The Systems View of Life* bridges the gap between biology, sociology, and ecology by fusing scientific knowledge with philosophical insight. It investigates the unity of all living forms, consistent with the concept that we are one. The book challenges readers to adopt a comprehensive perspective and to think about the symbiosis that keeps life on Earth possible. It offers a framework for seeing the Earth as a sophisticated, self-regulating system, motivating behavior based on systems theory.

Resurgence & Ecologist

The depth of cultural and spiritual investigation is combined with the urgency of ecological challenges in this magazine. It provides insightful information on anything from indigenous wisdom to climate action. For those who think that humans and the environment can coexist peacefully, resurgence is a perpetual source of inspiration as it reflects the spirit of regeneration. It highlights the importance of taking environmental action in addition to supporting cultural rejuvenation.

Schumacher College – Sustainable Curriculum

Schumacher College in Devon, England provides a distinctive educational philosophy that prioritizes deep ecology, holistic thinking, and sustainable living. The institution promotes learning that feeds the mind and the heart through classes and workshops. In addition to imparting knowledge, it inspires students to live as stewards of the planet. Schumacher College is a crucial resource for anyone looking to incorporate ecological consciousness into real-world action.

Braiding Sweetgrass

Robin Wall Kimmerer's book *Braiding Sweetgrass* presents a potent picture of the reciprocity that exists between people and the natural environment by fusing scientific knowledge with indigenous wisdom. It touches our hearts and teaches us that in order to restore the Earth, we must have gratitude and respect for the natural world. Kimmerer's work serves as a reminder that sustainability is a call to integrate many modes of knowledge and is as much about cultural resurrection as it is about ecological restoration.

Living with Fire

The documentary *Living with Fire* examines how human settlements and wildfire-prone environments have changed over time. It draws attention to contemporary fire safety measures, native customs, and the need for a more thorough comprehension of fire as a natural force. This resource, which is in line with the larger themes of resilience and coexistence in a changing climate, highlights the significance of learning from traditional knowledge and adapting to the shifting environment.

Your Pristine Blueprint

This book explores the idea of human potential and provides guidance on how people might connect with their greatest calling. In *Your Pristine Blueprint* by Beth McDougal M.D., personal progress is examined as a way to support the planet's and society's broader regeneration. It is consistent with *Dare To Evolve's* philosophy, which exhorts readers to welcome personal development as a component of a larger group movement toward a sustainable future.

The Virus and the Host

Dr. Chris Chlebowski, in *The Virus and the* Host explores how human interactions with ecosystems might result in resilience or vulnerability by examining the delicate balance between human activities and the microbial world. It acts as a reminder of the indissoluble connection between human health and the health of the world. Making plans for a future in which ecological integrity is not sacrificed for human progress requires an understanding of this relationship.

Becoming Supernatural

In his book *Becoming Supernatural*: How Common People Are Doing the Uncommon, Dr. Joe Dispenza examines the relationship between consciousness, quantum physics, and neuroscience to show how people can rewire their biology for transformation and healing and escape restrictive habits. Using these techniques Dr. Dispenza restored his own life. He experienced a life-threatening accident and his doctors told him he would never walk again. Dispenza demonstrates how concentrated intention and higher emotional states may produce quantifiable changes in the body and surroundings through scientific data, real-life tales, and guided approaches. The book is both inspirational and educational, urging readers to use their minds to influence reality, build resilience, and promote mental, emotional, and higher-consciousness congruence.

Why These Resources Matter

These literary pieces provide a path for individuals who aim to enhance their comprehension of and interaction with the world. They give viewpoints that question the status quo and inspire optimism for fresh opportunities. By embracing these resources readers can continue their path toward an evolved and regenerative life that is in line with sustainability, interconnection, and the timeless beauty of the natural world.

Every reference in this book serves not only as a source of knowledge but also as a roadmap towards the goal of a planet where all life coexists peacefully. By promoting a call to action and a deeper awareness, these materials pave the way for a more resilient and conscientious future. Together, let's keep learning, growing, and evolving.

Statistics to Investigate

*"Statistics can lie, but most correlations
need to be investigated."*

~ UNKNOWN

Data is our beacon in a world where the wellbeing of the Earth and its inhabitants is under rising danger. Promoting workable solutions requires an understanding of the scope and depth of the issues we face, from combat devastation to environmental degradation and public health concerns. The United States average age at death has declined to approximately 76 years. This is one example of a statistic that makes us want to know more. The following information demonstrates the urgency of our work and shows that the moment to act is now. The actual statistics are not listed here to encourage you to do your own research. Spend some time investigating the statistics in the following areas to get a sense of the problems that sustainable solutions address. You can look at the references to find more information.

1. Water Pollution Problems – (1950 – 2023)
Our freshwater systems quality has been rapidly declining as a result of untreated wastewater, agricultural runoff, and industrial pollutants. Pollutants like microplastics, nitrates, and heavy metals have increased since 1950, endangering both human health and ecosystems. The data is overwhelming: water pollution is a growing issue

that needs to be addressed immediately and sustainably. Its effects range from decreased biodiversity to contaminated drinking water. One example is plastic production from 1950 to 2019:

We don't need a chart to see how much plastic is polluting our water, our soil, and the air. We only need to look around as we walk almost anywhere to see the plastic waste that is not being remediated. There are many other water pollution problems, but this example shows how we are not caring for our water sources which are essential for life and the health of everyone on the planet.

2. Climate Pollution Problems (1950-2023)

Global temperatures have reached previously unheard-of heights due to the rise in greenhouse gas emissions, including carbon dioxide, since 1950. A few of the effects include extreme weather occurrences, melting ice caps, and rising sea levels. The information emphasizes the urgency of cutting emissions and switching to renewable energy sources. Not only are climate solutions pressing but they are also necessary for our survival.

3. Autism and the Use of Chemicals (1950-2023)

There is serious worry about the relationship between the rise in autism diagnoses and the increased use of chemicals in manufacturing and agriculture. Diagnoses of autism began to rise in the middle of the 20th century, at the same time as industrial chemicals and synthetic pesticides became widely used. Even though a link does not always imply a cause, this information raises interesting questions about potential environmental effects on brain health. It makes the case for the necessity for more hygienic production procedures, stringent laws, and a moving toward organic and regenerative farming practices that reduce exposure to dangerous chemicals.

4. Chronic Disease and the Use of Chemicals (1950-2023)

An alarming increase in the use of chemicals in food production, household items, and industrial waste has coincided with a sharp rise in chronic diseases like diabetes, asthma, and autoimmune disorders. According to the findings, diseases that were once uncommon are becoming more ubiquitous as our exposure to manmade chemicals increases. Given that what we put in our soil, air, and water directly affects human health, this calls for a renewed emphasis on lowering environmental toxins and implementing ecological alternatives.

5. Chronic Disease and Processed Food (1950-2023)

The correlation between nutrition and health is apparent when considering the growth in chronic illnesses associated with the increased intake of processed foods. Global diets have changed since 1950 due to the advent of artificial chemicals, preservatives, and high-sugar, low-nutrient foods. Convenience has come at a heavy cost, though, as rates of obesity, metabolic disorders, and heart disease are on the rise. By bringing attention to these figures, we hope to emphasize the significance of going back to eating complete, nutrient-dense foods, supporting methods that improve soil health, and advocating for a more nutritionally balanced diet.

6. Obesity and Processed Food (1950-2023)

The mass manufacture and marketing of processed foods, which are high in harmful fats and refined sugars and have become staple foods in many regions of the world, is intimately linked to the rise in obesity rates worldwide. The data clearly demonstrates a trend: obesity and accompanying diseases like Type 2 diabetes became more common as processed food became more widely available. This link highlights the need for moving toward natural, unprocessed foods and emphasizes how local, sustainable food systems may help create healthier communities.

7. Alzheimer's and Chemical Exposure (1950-2023)

The escalation of Alzheimer's disease and other neurodegenerative disorders coincides with heightened vulnerability to specific environmental contaminants, including air pollution, pesticides, and heavy metals. Research indicates that these substances may be involved in cognitive deterioration, which begs the question of what effects they may have on our aging society in the long run. The figures push us to decrease hazardous exposures, support clean air and water, and investigate the possibility of regenerative practices to bring balance back to our ecosystems as we work to create a world that supports healthy aging.

8. Global Trends Through Gapminder and Factfulness

With the help of tools like Gapminder and "Factfulness," we are able to see global patterns in income, health, and resource distribution from a wider angle. These tools give users a visual understanding of how successes in some areas contrast with failures in others. They aid our comprehension of the complexity of global development and the imperative to strike a balance between environmental stewardship and economic prosperity. These resources' data reveals that whereas some regions have advanced greatly, others are still having difficulty due to inequality and environmental damage.

9. Lack of Peace

Since the end of World War II, there have been no less than 26 active conflicts throughout the world. With the advent of chemical and nuclear weapons, we are capable of destroying all livable conditions on the planet. This has brought us to the point where we should be opting for peace and adopting a behavior that moves us beyond war. If we are to survive as a species, we must take every conflict seriously and seek diplomatic solutions to prevent escalations that could end everything.

A Call to Action

These statistics are more than just numerical data, they tell tales of opportunity, challenge, and transformation. They offer the chance for us to understand how our decisions affect both the health of our world and ourselves. We can work toward solutions that respect the natural world that sustains us while still acknowledging our desire for advancement by being aware of these patterns. The *Dare To Evolve* journey is an invitation to take these realizations to heart and welcome a future in which sustainability is a need rather than an option.

Diversity

"Strength lies in differences, not in similarities."

~ STEPHEN R. COVEY
Everyone Contributes Something

A vibrant, dynamic society is built on diversity. Regardless of their ethnic, racial, religious, gender, or generational perspectives, each person has something special to offer. This diversity increases creativity, opens up new ideas, and improves teamwork.

Cultural Diversity: Traditions, values, and a multitude of information are found in every culture. We can promote world unity and deepen our awareness of the world by accepting these disparities.

Racial Diversity: Diversity in race teaches us about resiliency, the strength of unity in adversity, and the grace of human flexibility. Respecting the histories and experiences that define each group is a necessary part of embracing racial differences.

Religious Diversity: Spirituality and religious activities influence morals and worldviews. Recognizing the multiplicity of religions fosters compassion and tolerance, which contribute to the development of societies in which people of all faiths can live in harmony.

Gender Diversity: Gender diversity expands our understanding of identity by letting go of traditional norms. We promote a society that relates to each individual by recognizing this spectrum. That said, we should be protecting children until they are of an age to make such an important decision.

Age Diversity: Young people and old people have different perspectives to contribute; one comes from a world of potential for the future, while the other is based on a lifetime of experiences. They combine wisdom and innovation in a balanced way.

Sexual Orientation: Sexual orientation is an essential component of an individual's identity, and every person's identity is valid. Acknowledging this promotes equality and guarantees that love is honored in all of its manifestations.

Disability Diversity: Individuals with impairments contribute unique perspectives on creativity and problem-solving. Ensuring everyone participates fully helps us to uncover innovative solutions that are advantageous to society as a whole.

Imagine – John Lennon

John Lennon asks us to imagine a world without boundaries related to religion, nationality, or materialism in his well-known song Imagine. It presents a positive image of people living in harmony and unity despite their diversity. Diversity envisions a society in which our differences serve as the threads that bind us together rather than tearing us apart.

Diversity Makes Us Stronger

We get stronger the more variety we welcome. Our differences spur innovation, encourage teamwork, and pave the way for a more compassionate and just world. Resilience is made possible by diversity in society, as each individual's distinct experiences combine to create a collective intelligence that can address the problems of the day.

Becoming

In her autobiography *Becoming* Michelle Obama describes her experiences navigating many environments as a Black woman, discovering her voice, and evolving into the person she is today. It demonstrates how our trajectories are shaped by the diversity of our experiences, backgrounds, and identities. *Becoming* is a call to recognize that we are constantly changing and our diversity is an essential component of who we are.

Building Bridgers – Peace and Collaboration

Depending on how we handle it, diversity may either be a cause of conflict or a spark for harmony. Creating connections between disparate groups encourages cooperation and respect for one another. Its more than a simply a notion. Building Bridgers is an active process that promotes communication, understanding, and empathy in order to create a world in which variety can lead to peace.

Van Jones work to get the justice reform bill passed is a good example of what it takes to work with people with whom we typically disagree.

References

References can be found at **www.daretoevolve.us**

KEY NAMES AND TERMINOLOGY

A/B C/D
Aclima
Agroforestry
Airbus
Algramo
Altars of Power and Grace (book)
 American Forest Foundation
Ametek
Angelou, Maya
Appalachia Water Project
The Art of Happiness (book)
Attenborough, Sir David
Audi
Axopar Boats
Babylonstoren (South Africa)
BAE Systems
Baker Creek Heirloom Seeds
Bakker, Joost
Ballymaloe Cookery School (Ireland)
Becoming (book)
Berry, Wendell
Beyond War (movement)
big AG
The Biggest Little Farm (CA) (Apricot Lane Farms)
bio-resonance
bio-optimization
Black Kestrel
Blue Zones

BMW
Bonneau, Anne-Marie
Brach, Tara PhD
Braiding Sweetgrass (book)
Breakthrough: Emerging New Thinking (book)
Building Bridgers
Building Bridges
Bush, Zach MD
Cape Dutch farm
Capra, Fritjof
Celebrate Your Divinity (book)
Charity: Water
Chlebowski, Dr. Chris
Cho, Fujio
Clean Water Action
CLEAR Center of Health
Colonias Water Project
The Compassion Project
Correct Craft
Covey, Stephen R.
Creative Education Foundation (CEF)
Creativity, Culture and Education (CCE)
Deep Time Walk
Diamond Aircraft
DigDeep
Down to Earth (documentary series)
Drakenstein Valley

E/F G/H

Earth (referring to the planet)

ECOsmarte

Effortless Mind (book)

e-Genius

Elco Motor Yachts

Elders Action Network

Electrek (website)

electrolyzers

The European Marine Energy Centre (EMEC)

Extended Producer Responsibility (EPR)

Extinction Rebellion (XR)

Factfulness (book?)

Farmer's Footprint

Flora Farms (Mexico)

Ford Electric

Foundation for Critical Thinking

The Freshwater Trust

Fridays for Future

futurefoodsystem

Gandhi, Mahatma

Gapminder

General Motors

The Global Interdependence Coalition

Global Wind Energy Council (GWEC)

Good Energy (book)

The Greatest Achievement (book)

Green New Deal

Gromyko, Anatoly

Haramein, Nassim

HeartMath Institute

Hellman, Martin

Henderson, Hazel PhD

Hepburn, Audrey

Honeywell

How to Talk to a Climate Skeptic (web series?)

Honda

Hyundai

I/J/K L/M

Institute of Noetic Sciences

Integrative Medicine: A Clinician's Journal

Intergovernmental Panel on Climate Change (IPCC)

International Cities of Peace

International Space Federation

Intravenous Vitamin C Protocol

Jahren, Hope

Jampolsky, Gerald MD

Jarman, Beth PhD

Johnson, Bea

Jones, Van

JYZEN Labs

Kaur, Valarie

Karen Harwell: Never Been Here Before (film)

Khan Academy

Kia

Kimmerer, Robin Wall

King, Dr. Martin Luther Jr.

Kiss the Ground

Klein, Naomi
Land, George PhD
LEED certification
(Leadership in Energy and
Environmental Design)
A Life on Our Planet (Netflix
film)
Lifewater International ?
"Water for Good" merger?
*Living Beyond War: A Citizens
Guide* (book)
Living With Fire
(documentary)
Loop
Lucid
Luisi, Pier Luigi
Lush Cosmetics
magniX
Margulies, Nancy
McCloskey, Diedre PhD
McClure, Kerry
McDougall, Beth MD
Mclean, Katie
Means, Casey MD
Mederi Center
Mercedes Electric
Mind to Matter (book)
Mirror In The Earth (book)
M.K. Gandhi Institute for
Nonviolence
Mount Shasta (CA)
Musk, Elon

N/O P/Q
NanoTech Materials ?
The National Renewable

Energy Laboratory (NREL)
Nature (scientific journal)
Navajo Water Project
The Need to Grow (documentary)
Net Zero Carbon Buildings
Commitment
Nissan
no-till farming (from no-tillage)
Oak Mountain Farm (OR)
Obama, Michelle
On Being / The On Being Project
*On Fire: The (Burning)
Case for a Green New Deal*
(book)
Parker Pastures (CO)
Patrick, Lyn ND
Pay-As-You-Throw (PAYT)
Peace Corps
peacebuilding (as one word)
Physicians for Social
Responsibility (PSR)
Pizzorno, Joseph ND
Plug In America
Polman, Paul
Polestar
Polyface Farms (VA)
Portland State University
Practical Wellness

R/S T/U
Radical Compassion (book)
RAIN protocol (Recognize,
Allow, Investigate,
Nurture)
The Reality We Create (book)
Regeneration International

Regenerative Organic Certified
Resnick, Mitchel
Resonant Technologies Group
Resurgence & Ecologist
(magazine)
The Revolutionary Love Project
Rifkin, Jeremy
Riordan Clinic
Rivian
Rocky Mountain Institute
(RMI)
Rogue Valley Heritage Grain
Project
Roosevelt, Franklin D.
Sage Warrior (book)
Safran
Salatin, Joel (Polyface Farms)
Save the California Delta ?
"Restore the Delta"?
Schumacher College
Sea Hugger
See No Stranger (book)
Seed Savers Exchange
sickness care (alternative phrase
to "healthcare")
Sierra de la Laguna Mountains
Singing Frogs Farm (CA)
Ski Nautique E
Snake River (ID)
Steiner, Rudolf
Sunrise Movement
Sustainable House (Sydney,
Australia)
The Systems View of Life (book)
Tabula Rasa Farms (OR)
Tesla

Thales
*The Third Industrial
Revolution* (book)
Thunberg, Greta
Tippett, Krista
Twain, Mark
Twelve Principles of
Attitudinal Healing
Udemy
UN Global Compact
UnderstandingAG
University of Stuttgart
UpTerra
U.S. Environmental
Protection Agency (EPA)
U.S. Green Building Council
(USGBC)

V/W X/Y/Z
Vastu
Vesper Meadow (OR)
Vivekananda, Swami
Volkswagen
Volvo
WasteZero Solutions
Water for Good (merged
with Lifewater International)
Water For People
The Water Project
WaterCredit Initiative
Water.org
well-being
Wild Minds Community
William Holden Wildlife
Foundation (Kenya)

WiTricity
The World Bank
World BEYOND War
World Green Building
Council (WorldGBC)
Your Pristine Blueprint
(book)
Zero Emissions Research and
Initiatives (ZERI)
Zero Waste Europe
Zero Waste Home (book and
website)
Zero Waste International
Alliance
ZeroWaste.Org

PEOPLE
Angelou, Maya
Attenborough, Sir David
Bakker, Joost
Berry, Wendell
Bonneau, Anne-Marie
Brach, Tara PhD
Bush, Zach MD
Capra, Fritjof
Chlebowski, Chris ND
Cho, Fujio
Covey, Stephen R.
Dispenza, Joe DC
Gandhi, Mahatma
Gromyko, Anatoly
Haramein, Nassim
Harwell, Karen
Hellman, Martin
Henderson, Hazel PhD

Hepburn, Audrey
Jahren, Hope
Jampolsky, Gerald MD
Jarman, Beth PhD
Johnson, Bea
Jones, Van
Kaur, Valarie
Kimmerer, Robin Wall
King, Dr. Martin Luther Jr.
Klein, Naomi
Land, George PhD
Luisi, Pier Luigi
Margulies, Nancy
McCloskey, Diedre PhD
McClure, Kerry
McDougall, Beth MD
Mclean, Katie
Means, Casey MD
Means Rob
Musk, Elon
Obama, Michelle
Patrick, Lyn ND
Pizzorno, Joseph ND
Polman, Paul
Resnick, Mitchel
Rifkin, Jeremy
Roosevelt, Franklin D.
Salatin, Joel
Steiner, Rudolf
Suler, Asia
Thunberg, Greta
Tippett, Krista
Twain, Mark
Vivekananda, Swami

Acknowledgments

My best instructor has been nature. I am reminded that nothing is out of place when I observe a flower in silence, a spider's delicate web, or the rhythm of the creek running through the park. Everything has a place. I hear the whisper of togetherness when I listen with presence. I recall who I am in that resonance. We are one.

Kerry McClure — my companion in everything, your love uplifts me. I am called to my higher self by your unfailing support and profound examination, particularly when I lose sight of what is possible.

To my daughter, Jenna Hales — whose love endures despite dispute. I am humbled by the courage you exhibit. I appreciate you spotting the chaos and assisting in quietening it. I feel the love in your support.

To Asia Suler — for writing in a way that inspired and stirred me to take a chance and create this book. Your ability to explain and craft the picture in the mind of that subject or experience with clarity and motivational energy has enabled a new side of me.

To Valarie Kaur — whose book *See No Stranger* was another catalyst in igniting my writing desire. Your adoption of "Revolutionary Love" provides a hope that gives our world a way forward embracing the only true solution. Love everyone as we love ourselves.

Cory Ross — your vision at Vesper Meadows is a light. My own journey toward renewal is inspired by the way you have respect for the soil.

To Donnie Yance — I appreciate your intense questioning and the insight it provides. My path has become sharper thanks to your talent for separating truth from complexity.

Jennifer Yance — your tools, wisdom, and sincere concern helped me sort through some of the confusion. I appreciate your faith in what I'm creating.

MaryAnn Marks — I value your brilliant suggestions and heartfelt support. You are a compass because of your bright mind and giving nature. Experiencing your soul is a life highlight for me.

Tina Cole — your vibe is a warm welcome. I appreciate you adding excitement, happiness, humor, and celebration to the trip. Keep being excited.

Meme Mae Curtis — you are a bright light with your knowledge of homeschooling and unconventional teaching methods. You serve as a reminder to me of the importance of taking care of the child and the entire world through providing discerning alternatives.

Greg Conaway — your insightful advice and extensive experience enhanced the caliber of this work. I appreciate you sharpening the edge.

Mira Dessy — thank you for helping to make the tumultuous world of book production feel manageable. You enabled more clarity.

To Marilyn Lindsay — You exude soul through your dedication to education. I appreciate you standing up for the ultimate good.

Chris Millia — your inquiries led me to more fertile ground. I appreciate you igniting a deeper comprehension.

Lisa Francesca — your comments were enlightening and helpful. In addition, your family story, which was so honest and relatable, made me realize why we write at all. Thank you for your inspiration.

Thank you to Parthenia Hicks — your practical expertise and understanding provided this path to publishing with depth and scope. I appreciate what you contributed and sharing additional resources.

Rob Means — for educating me on the need for the last mile transportation in congested and high traffic cities. Seeing the ability for timely and convenient passage clearly gives us hope for adjusting our infrastructure to serve and at the same time enable natural solutions.

To Ginger McClure — for having the interest of furthering my efforts. You provided connections that have made this a better creation.

Thank you, Anik Bose — for your consistent clarity and selfless contribution. Your ability to always add value is appreciated and brought a simple intelligence with precision to the preface.

To my editor, Sasha Dessy, PhD — whose insight and understanding enabled me to make this book a reality. You honored the passion underlying the words, and have made them better. Thank you.

Chris Molé — Thank you for a design that enables the intended message of this book. Your expertise has added an exciting invitation of readability that captures a new imagination. I am grateful.

Christopher Briscoe — I would like to thank you for sharing your experience on the publishing journey. Your continued interest has been inspiring.

To Irv Lubliner — sharing your experience with your mother's book and the challenges you were able to overcome lifted me to believe that it was possible for me.

Please pardon me if I've forgotten somebody. Creation is never a genuinely solitary endeavor; rather, it is a network, supported by numerous hands. I appreciate each and every one of you.

About the Author

I am an advocate for sustainable alternatives. Our history of improving human existence for the most part has been in dissonance, making decisions mostly for acquiring money rather than opting for less harmful alternatives. Coal for heat and electricity, oil and gas to power automobiles, chemicals to control insects and weeds, our propensity for continuous conflict. All of these choices have created a space where our health and well-being are in peril. I see great challenges facing us that are unprecedented in my lifetime. With these challenges come great opportunities. I believe that no matter what our circumstances, we have the ability to add value with our talents, our enthusiasm, our knowledge, and our caring. All the while asking: do I need to change my mind to enable a better aligned solution?

We are living on the cusp of a potential for a new paradigm where we develop novel and exciting technologies to enhance human health and wellbeing using new physics that is in resonance, and support new potentials only heretofore thought to be science fiction. The website https://spacefed.com/ is one source of information on these new possibilities.

My website on sustainability www.sustainall.us covers a number of areas where I believe we are going to be able to embrace sustainable solutions to change the trajectory of the current challenges we face. Most of those on my site are also covered in this book.

Also, I enjoy all technology. I started programming computers in 1965 and have been an advocate of technologies that carry us toward better communication and collaboration.

www.ingramcontent.com/pod-product-compliance
Lightning Source LLC
Chambersburg PA
CBHW071240130626
46556CB00003B/1101